Get What You REALLY Want

Without the GUILT

*This book shows you how to release your brakes, overcome your
limitations and achieve your full potential!*

> —BRIAN TRACY, author of *Change Your Thinking, Change Your Life*

*Sandra Smith's wisdom and story-telling ability, along with her
powerful step-by-step processes for learning more about yourself
and breaking through your limitations, will help you to create just
the life you want.*

> —NORMA CARR-RUFFINO, Ph.D. Professor of Management,
> San Francisco State University, author of *The Promotable Woman*

*Sandra Smith has a special way of touching the reader straight to
the soul through the words in this book. When you read it expect to
be transformed spiritually and emotionally. It is a must read.*

> —DR. KIMBERLY VENTUS-DARKS, International Motivator
> and Author, The Dr. Kim Experience, LLC

*Get What You Really Want...offers guidance, action plans, and
first-hand insights from someone who has worked to make the
changes required for success. If you are ready to get what you really
want in life, this book is for you.*

> —SUNNY KOBE COOK, Author/Speaker/Award-Winning Entrepreneur

*I have attended many management training programs, leadership
conferences, and technical training seminars throughout my thirty-
year career in the field, and I can honestly say that you are one of
the best, if not the best, Facilitator I've encountered.*

> —DAVE KOLAKOWSKI, Senior Director, Corporate Training, Hawaiian Airlines

*I would recommend you highly to anyone who asked. You are
humorous, entertaining, and creative in your approach. We can't
wait to have you back.*

> —TAMMY L. SULLIVAN, Employee Involvement Facilitator, The Boeing Company

*I can attest to the fact that EVERYONE who attended came away
feeling refreshed and inspired. It has been several months since our
event and we continue to laugh and talk about the pearls of wisdom
you left with us.*

> —SHARON DESMOND, Manager, Department of Health, National Cancer Institute

Entertaining, inspirational, and moving!

> —DANA PETHIA, Membership Development Officer, Twin County Credit Union

Sandra's techniques and the simple tools she shared are working; our employees still talk about the seminar and the positive effect it has had on them. I highly recommend Sandra's services.

—LORNE SANFORD, MS, Regional Administrator, Dept. of Labor and Industries

In the salon business, communication is everything. Not only did you help us to understand how to better communicate, you gave us a forum to learn about each other.

—Michelle Arnold, Salon Coordinator, 14th and Grand Salon

Thank you for your passion and dedication to providing training to state, city, and county employees. We know that the attendees come away with both practical and useable information that they can apply in both their professional and personal lives. You definitely make a difference to those who attend your training classes.

—Wendy Sue Wheeler, Former Education Committee Co-Chair, ICSEW

The young women we work with are difficult because of their negative and self-defeating attitudes. They were all ready to put down your presentation and turn it into a bad experience. However, your personable, enthusiastic, and "real" approach completely disarmed them. They were blown away by your presentation on feelings and "flipping your card."

—Jill Sharp, Ed.M, Clinical Supervisor, Faith Homes

As I walk through the offices, I see many of Sandra's ideas posted on boards to remember when waiting on customers to give the best customer service possible.

—Carolyn Randall, Field Services Coordinator, Department of Labor and Industries

Foster youth are often called "America's forgotten population." Please know how grateful we are that you have chosen to remember and support these young people, who often feel that no one understands their plight. Your presentation was well-received and very helpful to the clients we serve.

—Va Lecia Adams, Ph.D., Director, United Friends of the Children

I can tell that you have a passion for what you do and that is why you do it so well. You speak with great enthusiasm that captures your audience!

—Jeanne Wasserman, Manager, Alameda County Fairgrounds

Get
What You
REALLY
Want

Without the GUILT

How to Ignite Energy,
Create Motivation *and*
Conquer Stress *for* Success

SANDRA SMITH

ASPIRE
SEMINARS
PUBLISHERS

Unattributed quotations are by Sandra Smith.

Library of Congress Cataloging-in-Publication Data
    Smith, Sandra.
    Get What You Really Want Without the Guilt: How to Ignite Energy,
    Create Motivation, and Conquer Stress for Success
    Includes bibliographical references and appendix.
    ISBN-13: 978-0-9786764-0-7
    ISBN-10: 0-9786764-0-8
        1. Change (Psychology)
        2. Success—Psychological aspects.

Aspire Seminars Publishers' books and workbooks are available at special discounts to corporations, professional associations, and educational and other organizations. For details, contact Aspire Seminars Special Markets, PO Box 3603, Lacey, WA 98509-3603.

Cover design by George Foster
Author photograph by Tasha Owen
Editing by Barbara Fandrich
Page Design by Kathryn E. Campbell
Printed in the United States of America

First edition

ASPIRE
SEMINARS

PUBLISHERS

This book is dedicated to my son, Jared, and

to the memory of my mom and dad,
Dorie and Al.

Thanks...

To Oprah Winfrey who encourages all
of us to keep going no matter what.

To all of the women and men who have shared
their life stories with me.

To the wonderful crew who collaborated
on the making of this book.

To Bob who kept everything in motion so I could keep going.

To my many guardian angels who take such good care of me.

I am blessed to be able to write and publish my work.

Contents

Is This Book for You?

*T*his book was written for busy people who feel stuck, stressed, and want more out of life. If you are looking for energy, motivation, and the path to your destiny, then this book is for you.

The subject matter of this book is driven by eleven "why" questions. I believe that most of your frustration and stress comes from not being able to find answers to these questions. I know the answers, when you find them, can be life-changing.

Here are the eleven questions:

ELEVEN POWERFUL QUESTIONS

1   Why can't I believe in myself?

2   Why do I even get up in the morning?

3   Why can't I change?

4   Why can't I get out of my comfort zone?

5   Why are people hard to deal with?

6   Why do I get stuck in my negative emotions?

7   Why can't I get rid of my fear?

8   Why can't I motivate myself?

9   Why can't I conquer clutter?

10   Why can't I get stuff done?

11   Why am I so stressed-out?

If you identified with any of the "why" questions, help is on the way. Each question has a corresponding chapter that is filled with exercises, ideas, and strategies to help you overcome your challenges.

I describe this book as part self-help and part how-to, which I think is the best of both worlds. It is written in a nonlinear layout so you can read any chapter you want in any order you want.

I wrote this book when I realized that most people are still looking for their life's purpose. My specialty and passion is to help you do just that. Remember, every time you ask why, seek the answers to those questions. The answers will help you discover your purpose.

Introduction

*L*et me begin by asking you, do you ever feel as if you're doing the same thing over and over and getting no further in life? Do you feel as if what you do doesn't matter? Are you stressed out and out of balance?

The purpose of this book is to help you get clarity on how to get unstuck, achieve what you want to achieve, and create a life that is successful because it is in alignment with your values and beliefs.

In *Get What You Really Want Without the Guilt* you will learn steps, secrets, and strategies on how to handle stress, the power of your thoughts, how enough is enough, how to speak up, and how to get stuff done even when you don't feel like it.

My advice to you as you begin this book is simply this: Get seriously committed to your success, and then a whole set of changes will be set in motion that you never thought possible.

As you read this book, you will be asked to do some new things. At times, you will feel challenged to stay motivated because you won't feel as if you're moving forward. Don't let that fool you into thinking you aren't changing, though, because you are—one choice at a time.

Your ability to succeed at your personal and professional goals will depend on your ability to effect change. I am not asking *you to change—because you are perfect the way you are. What I am asking you to change are some of your choices, your thoughts, and your habits.*

Just the idea of changing can freak most people out. I know it did me. In fact, most of my life I rejected the idea that I deserved success and I didn't even think I was capable of changing.

When I was little I had a terrible temper, I never completed anything, and I never succeeded at anything. When I became an adult, I failed at marriage, owning a business, making money, and my personal relationships.

I developed a reputation as someone who never stuck with anything. When I attended networking meetings, I would run into acquaintances who would smirk and say, "Last time we talked you had your own radio show. Now I hear you are off the air. How come?"

My reply was always the same: "I wasn't a good fit for the job." That was an understatement. I was fired from most of the jobs I had. If they didn't fire me, I would quit.

Ongoing failure can create a vicious cycle because the more you fail, the less you feel able to succeed. The less you feel able to succeed, the more you become consumed with fear and fear moves you away from your dreams and your true self.

In order to move forward, you must take the time necessary to look closely at your current choices, thoughts, and habits. This is important because self-knowledge helps us identify what is holding us back.

Not knowing who we are and why we do the things we do limits our access to crucial information that can help us grow. For it is in the moment of self-discovery that we make our greatest movement forward.

If you are someone who wants to get unstuck, achieve what you want to achieve, and create a life that is successful because it is in alignment with your values and beliefs, then *Get What You Really Want Without the Guilt* was written just for you.

$\mathscr{A}$spire to . . .

Live your life with passion and purpose;
know who you are, why you are here,
and where you are going;
find the meaning and reason for your life—and
at the end of your life know that you fulfilled your destiny.

ASPIRE
SEMINARS

1

═══ HOW TO ═══

Transform Beliefs

*F*or as long as I can remember I have wanted to be successful; however, the one thing in life I succeeded at was failure. Year after year I tried to run my own business, be financially secure, lose weight, and find love—only to fail. I lacked inner strength, energy, motivation, persistence, self-love, and self-esteem.

There is no doubt in my mind that I have always been my greatest obstacle to becoming successful and, for me, it was my negative self-limiting beliefs, and the feeling that I did not deserve what success would bring me, that kept me from living the life I was meant to live.

Unfortunately, it never occurred to me that as long as I continued to believe I was a failure, success would be out of my reach. It wasn't until I took responsibility for my own future, removed my own self-imposed obstacles, and believed I deserved success, that I finally found my path.

If you only have time to read one chapter, read this chapter. If down the road you start feeling unmotivated and believe you can't go after your dreams, come back to these pages and read them again. The purpose of this chapter is to help you develop your own personal inner strength so you can go after what you really want.

Take a moment and think about your life. What is it that you really want? What are your self-beliefs? Are they holding you back? What do you believe you deserve?

I believe my childhood contributed the most to my negative self-limiting belief system. When I was growing up, I was the child on which my father projected his anger. He had a terrible temper and constantly threatened to hurt me, and many times he did. I have no memory of my father ever telling me he loved me.

What I do remember is his never-ending negative criticism of everything I did. I can still hear his critical voice in my head, and I can still see the disgusted look on his face as he delivered his brutal remarks. Those memories are forever embedded in my mind.

When I grew up and got married, do you think I chose someone who was kind and loving? No, I picked a person who drank too much and became abusive, just like my father. As a result of that marriage, we had a baby.

Because of domestic violence, one Monday afternoon I bought two one-way tickets for my two-year-old son and me. It was that day my life changed forever. We flew to another state, with nothing but a suitcase, and started a new life completely from scratch.

Soon I found myself on welfare. While on welfare, I became fat, broke, scared of life, and fearful that I couldn't survive as a single mother. We lived in a dumpy, sparsely furnished apartment where I was often physically sick and so stressed out that my dentist informed me I had cracked a back tooth from stress biting.

I remember one day being at a checkout counter in a grocery store. The customer ahead of me turned around and looked at me, looked at my groceries, then looked at my baby in the cart. As I was getting out my food stamps he said, "Excuse me, can I ask you a question?" I said yes. He said, "I see you must be on welfare. You mean to tell me you can't find a job?"

I stood there, dazed. Then he said, "Lady, I'm going to make a prediction. You're a loser and that kid in the cart is going to be a loser." He continued, "And maybe you could find a job if you weren't so fat." I just stood there, unable to think or speak because I was so stunned by his words.

I finally got off of welfare and found a job. However, just about every job I was hired for I was fired from because I was so negative and disrespectful toward people. For a number of years, my average length of employment was about six months.

Back then, I got up every morning without any hope for a life I could love and went to jobs I absolutely hated, knowing inside I had considerable talent waiting to come out. I felt stuck and unhappy with my weight, my poverty-level income, and my lack of belief in myself.

My life changed, however, when I chose to replace believing that I was a failure with believing that I was becoming successful. When I went from feeling that I deserved nothing to believing that I deserved what my heart desired, I began to see myself in a new light and was able to create the life of my dreams.

In other words, when I stopped focusing on what I wanted and started focusing on who I needed to become, I found the path to my destiny. And since this book is about success, I guess you could say I ultimately succeeded at becoming the person I was truly meant to be.

Today I wake up everyday excited about my life. My passion is helping people find their personal paths to their destiny. As an author and speaker, I am able to reach and teach people the message of self-empowerment. I am sure you have read many great books on this topic; however, my goal is to present it to you in a fresh, new way using my personal stories and "how to" strategies.

It's customary for me to ask seminar attendees, "How many of you have something in your life you wish to achieve that you have not yet accomplished?" The results are shocking: almost everyone raises their hands!

If I can help you identify what you want, figure out what is holding you back from getting what you want, and create solutions to overcome your obstacles, I believe you will be well on your way to living the life of your dreams.

The purpose of this book is to help you develop your own personal inner strength so you can go after what you really want. This will not be an easy task. To make the process easier, I will help you create a *Get What You Really Want* Workbook.

Now would be a good time for you to get a three-ring binder. This binder will be a great place for you to work on all of the questions and exercises presented in each chapter. Make and label a section for each chapter, and then photocopy the work pages from the appendix to insert in each section. These work pages are found in the appendix ready for you to copy and place in your binder. You may want to insert some blank pages into each section for your notes and for chapter exercises as well.

Your *Get What You Really Want* Workbook will help you:

- Stay focused on what you want.
- Keep your momentum going.
- Record and review how much you have grown.

What do you really want? Do you want money, a beautiful home, the perfect job, love, balance, or a meaningful relationship? What is holding you back from getting what you really want? Is your obstacle fear, negativity, low self-esteem, procrastination, lack of choices, the need to please, stress, lack of time, or lack of money?

No matter where you're at today, you have the power to consciously choose to see yourself in a new light and create the life of your dreams. And when you live the life you really want, the feeling of being stuck and stressed will be replaced with energy and motivation.

It's time to get started. Before you begin, though, I would like to give you a few words of advice:

- Surround yourself with people you trust, people who have your best interest at heart.

- Buy a journal or customize your workbook; record all of your thoughts, ideas, and discoveries, and date your entries so you can track your progress.

- Never give up. Never.

I developed a three-step system to help you go from where you are to where you want to be, in order to get what you really want. The challenge of following this system will be to look for things in yourself you might not have seen before. You will experience three important benefits from doing this system:

1. You will identify what you really want.

2. You can figure out what is holding you back.

3. You will create solutions to overcome your obstacles.

Step 1: Identify What You Really Want

This initial step will help you answer these two important questions:

1. What are my beliefs and my life like now?

2. What do I want to change?

SECTION A: SELF-KNOWLEDGE QUESTIONNAIRE

The "Self-Knowledge Questionnaire" will help you see what your life and beliefs are like now and help you focus on what you want to change. Please answer yes or no to as many questions as you can. You can photocopy the questionnaire provided in the appendix of this book and insert it into your workbook.

Self-Knowledge Questionnaire

Yes No

____ ____ I feel I have too much stress in my life.

____ ____ I sleep too much or not enough.

____ ____ I overeat or do not eat enough.

____ ____ I look to others for approval.

____ ____ I constantly focus on things I cannot control.

____ ____ I feel stuck in my comfort zone.

____ ____ I wish I could control my emotions.

____ ____ Enough is never enough for me.

____ ____ I avoid conflict.

____ ____ I wish I could stop being a perfectionist.

____ ____ I take forever to make a decision because I lack confidence.

____ ____ I make a decision, and then replay my decision with regret.

____ ____ After an argument, I find it difficult to move on.

____ ____ I feel selfish when I ask for what I want.

____ ____ I feel an overwhelming sense of failure.

____ ____ I lack energy.

____ ____ I lack motivation.

____ ____ I stay with someone I no longer love.

____ ____ I constantly second-guess myself.

____ ____ I distract myself from my feelings by staying busy.

____ ____ I believe you should settle for what you already have.

____ ____ I take everything personally.

____ ____ I get stressed out when I procrastinate.

____ ____ I have physical clutter but feel unable to get rid of it.

____ ____ I hate my job but keep working there.

____ ____ I lose energy just thinking about an upcoming project.

____ ____ I hate the way my body looks.

____ ____ I can still hear the voice of my critical mother or father.

____ ____ I feel I lack time to do something just for me.

____ ____ I worry a lot.

____ ____ I feel lonely.

____ ____ I feel I lack emotional support.

____ ____ I am concerned with my finances.

____ ____ I engage in negative self-talk.

____ ____ It is hard to establish and maintain healthy relationships.

____ ____ I get embarrassed and/or disregard compliments.

____ ____ I hate getting older.

____ ____ I feel guilty when I ask for what I want or need.

____ ____ I am unable to deal with my fears.

____ ____ I blame myself when things go wrong.

SECTION B: ELIMINATING SELF-LIMITING BELIEFS

Now that the questionnaire is complete, I want you to write down on a sheet of paper all the statements on the questionnaire you answered with a yes. You can photocopy the appropriate page in the appendix of this book, and use the example below as a guide.

Each statement represents what you believe about yourself, and these beliefs have the potential to hold you back from your dreams. I love this list because it brings out into the open what you are really thinking on the inside. We have the capacity to conquer an obstacle when we become aware of it.

Negative Self-Limiting Beliefs

List the statements you recorded with a yes, such as these:

I feel stuck in my comfort zone.

I wish I could control my emotions.

I lack energy.

SECTION C: ACQUIRING SELF-EMPOWERING BELIEFS

Now that you have your list of negative self-limiting beliefs, I want you to rewrite each negative self-limiting belief into a positive self-empowering belief. You can use the sheet in the appendix that you have photocopied.

A positive self-empowering belief is simply a positive statement that states the outcome you want—whether you are currently that way or not. Your world is a reflection of your belief system, and whatever beliefs are more dominant in your thinking will be reflected outward into your daily life. Therefore, by becoming aware of negative self-limiting beliefs, then choosing to replace them with positive self-empowering beliefs, as shown in the example immediately below, you are in a position to change the outcome.

Acquiring Self-Empowering Beliefs

Negative Self-Limiting Beliefs	Positive Self-Empowering Beliefs
I feel stuck in my comfort zone.	*I am OK outside my comfort zone.*
I cannot control emotions.	*I feel my emotions, then I problem-solve.*
I lack energy.	*I am creating energy by doing.*

8

Step 1 Summary

- The questionnaire serves as a reflection of your inner strengths and limitations.

- The list of yes statements from the questionnaire serves as a reflection of possible obstacles for you.

- The rewritten yes statements from the questionnaire provide empowering thoughts and beliefs to help you overcome your obstacles.

Step 2: Figure Out What Is Holding You Back

This step will help you answer these two important questions:

1. Are my self-beliefs holding me back?

2. How are my self-beliefs holding me back?

SECTION D: IDENTIFYING LIMITATIONS

Look at the list you made of your Negative Self-Limiting Beliefs. For each statement, decide if the negative self-limiting belief is holding you back by answering yes or no. Now I want you to think about how the belief is holding you back; write down your thoughts. You can photocopy the page provided in the appendix and add it to your workbook. If you feel something on the list isn't holding you back, you can remove it because it would not be considered an obstacle for you at this time.

Identifying Limitations

What is my belief?	Is it holding me back?	How?
I lack energy.	*Yes.*	*I need energy to change.*
I am stupid.	*Yes.*	*It keeps me from trying.*

SECTION E: REWRITING SELF-BELIEFS

Now it is time to take action. When you rewrite a self-belief, and then act "as if" you already are different, you eventually become those qualities. For example, if you wrote, "I cannot control my emotions," and then rewrote it to read, "I feel my emotions, then I problem-solve," you are now becoming a problem-solver. The more you act "as if," you eventually will no longer be acting because you will have acquired a new behavior, and that new behavior will become a habit.

Step 2 Summary

- Any negative self-belief you can identify can be rewritten to a positive self-empowering belief.

- When you act "as if," you eventually acquire the change you seek.

- Overcoming your obstacles through problem-solving and taking action is the key to creating the life of your dreams.

Step 3: Create Solutions to Overcome Your Obstacles

The third step will help you answer these two important questions:

1. What is it that I want to have?

2. Who would I need to become in order to get what I want to have?

SECTION F: IDENTIFYING WHAT I WANT TO HAVE

Label a page for your workbook entitled "What I Want to Have," or photocopy the appropriate page in the appendix of this book. Write down everything you want to have. Just go crazy with it. It can be starting your own business, acquiring a new home, adapting a healthy lifestyle, or having more money.

What I Want to Have

My own business
A new home

SECTION G: BECOMING WHO I NEED TO BE

Now it is time to tackle the last question. Who would you need to become in order to get what you want to have? Most people look at what they want to have first. On the outside they say they want money, a new home, or own their own business. Inside, their negative self-belief system works against them and they wonder why they lack energy and motivation to go after what they really want. They neglect to consider who they would have to become in order to have what they want to have. When you turn it around and look at who you would need to be in order to have what you want to have, you empower yourself to go for your dreams. Over time you will experience inner peace when the results of your behavior meet your needs. For practice, pick one item from the want list you created in section F. Now ask yourself, who would I need to become in order to have what I want to have? You may photocopy the corresponding page from the appendix to write on and put into your workbook.

Becoming Who I Need to Be

I want to be: I want to be a business owner.

Be:	Do:	Have:
Focused	*Apply for a license*	*My own business*
Confident	*Attend training*	
Driven	*Create a logo*	
Self-directed	*Buy a computer*	

Step 3 Summary

- Know what you want.

- Know who you would need to become to have what you want to have.

- Think, feel, and act those qualities until they become a part of you.

Congratulations! You are done. I hope you found this chapter valuable. I recommend you redo the "Get What You Really Want" system about every six months. Save all your work pages in your workbook so you can track your progress. Before you go to chapter two, I would like to review the work you did in this chapter.

Review

Step 1, section A, had you fill out a questionnaire to show you what your life and beliefs are like now. This helps you focus on what you want to change.

In section B you created a "Negative Self-Limiting Belief" page from the items marked yes on the questionnaire. This page can serve as a mirror of the negative self-talk that goes on in your head.

Section C asked you to rewrite every negative self-limiting belief into a positive self-empowering belief. This is how you start to shed your old beliefs and begin to see yourself in a new light. It provides you with new behaviors and beliefs that support who you are becoming.

In step 2, section D, you were asked to review your "Negative Self-Limiting" page and decide if the beliefs on that page were holding you back or not. Then you were asked to write down how you feel each negative belief is holding you back. This exercise really puts you in a position to objectively see how your beliefs are holding you back.

Section E asked you to act "as if" you are already operating from the positive self-empowering beliefs you listed in section C. This speaks to the idea that you get to choose your thoughts, and then your actions will follow your thoughts. I am asking you to repeatedly think, say, and do your new positive beliefs over and over until they become a habit.

Finally, step 3, section F, asked you to write down everything you want to have. This helps you see what is missing in your life. For everything you want for yourself, you must believe you deserve it. If you don't believe you deserve it, you won't manifest it. It will help you to see how your beliefs are directly related to what you are able to manifest in your life.

Section G bridges that gap between who you are now and who you will need to be in order to have what you want to have. Let's say I decided I wanted to write a book, but I always felt I was too stupid to be an author. I would need to see myself as capable and intelligent to accomplish writing a book. You must empower yourself with a personal inner strength that says you can do it.

Every desire that has been placed in your heart was put there to guide you to your true self, and only by being yourself can you truly achieve your dreams. Trust your destiny.

Sandra's Success Secrets

Having no hope of changing those things
we want to change can lower our energy and
motivation and increase our stress.

It takes energy and motivation
to overcome life's challenges.

Every time we fail at trying to change,
it can deepen our sense of worthlessness.

2

HOW TO

Ignite Energy

*T*his book is about how to increase your energy and motivation to get what you really want. A great place to start is to realize you must have a purpose or compelling reason to get up in the morning and do more than just get through another day.

If you are like a lot of people, however, you get up in the morning with a long list of things you need to do and no time to pursue what you want to do. At the end of the day you go to bed exhausted, only to get up the next day and do it all over again.

It is almost impossible to find energy and motivation to go after your dreams when you are stressed out and distracted from what's important to you. When your life is too busy to engage in activities that are personally satisfying, you can end up feeling disconnected from your own life.

Take a look at what your typical day looks like. I would like you to create a "My Life Today" sheet for your workbook. Make two columns. The first column will contain everything you have to do in a day. The second column will contain everything you want to do but can't because you lack time, energy, or resources. You may photocopy the page from the appendix of this book.

My Life Today

I do	I want to do
_____	_____
_____	_____
_____	_____
_____	_____
_____	_____

Can you see why it is a challenge to find your purpose? For instance, you want to exercise but can't find the time, so you don't exercise. You want to clear out clutter but you lack energy, so you don't clear out the clutter. All those undone activities keep adding up. No wonder you end up without energy and motivation!

It can be hard to move forward when you can't find a way to do more of what you want to do and less of what you don't want to do. The big question is this: How can you start doing more of what you want to do if you lack time, energy, and motivation?

That is a great question to ask because doing what you really want to do usually aligns with your life's purpose. I am hoping this book helps you find answers so you can stop wondering when your purpose will show up and learn how to pursue it with a vengeance.

It is important for you to ask yourself these questions and it is worth putting time in to get the answers because knowing your life's purpose has many benefits. It becomes a beacon guiding you to your destiny, it helps you stay on your path when times get tough, and it *is* the reason for you to get up in the morning.

Before we talk about how to find your life's purpose, I want to talk about what can hold you back. Here are the three beliefs that can keep you stuck, stressed, and unable to tap into your internal energy and motivation:

1. You don't believe you have choices; in other words, you believe your life has to be the way it is and nothing is going change.

2. You don't believe you have the power to get what you want.

3. You don't believe you deserve what it is you are going after.

My personal belief is that in order for you to find and live a purposeful life, you need to believe you have choices, believe you can get what you want, and believe you deserve it. The good news is now you know what can potentially hold you back and what you need to focus on to make your dreams come true.

Why don't you grab your workbook, take a moment, and ask yourself where you stand on these three beliefs. How many times have you said to yourself that your life is the way it is and it's not going to change so why try? What do you believe you have the power to do? What do you believe you deserve?

I hope you spent some time in chapter one and found some helpful ideas on how to think about and work with your personal belief system, which should make this chapter a little easier to work through.

Take it easy on yourself if you don't know the answers to the belief questions. They sound easy to answer, but they are not. Often you are so busy just surviving another day that you aren't afforded the luxury of time to focus on thriving for a better tomorrow.

Now that you know what can hold you back from finding your life's purpose, it's time to find out what a "purpose" is and how to acquire it. Get your workbook out and get ready to write.

Purpose can be described as a picture you see in your mind that provides a clear and challenging vision of where you are going. A purpose connects you with having a sense of your destiny.

When you find your purpose, you will also ignite your passion. Passion and purpose are sisters and they love hanging out together.

I want you to go after and find your purpose with great excitement. To help you do that, I have created a process that has three steps. Learn the ones you need to learn, do the ones you need to do; they don't have to be carried out in any particular order.

In your workbook, label this section "Finding My Purpose." Then, label the next three pages with these three steps: Purposeful Thinking, Purposeful Choices, and Purposeful Doing.

Step 1: Purposeful Thinking

Purposeful thinking means that you become aware of your thoughts. You can then delete thoughts that are negative and create thoughts that empower you.

Purposeful thinking can be particularly difficult to do because it takes a high level of consciousness to think a thought, and then convert it to a message that is empowering. And it takes a high level of trust to think a thought and believe it can serve you in a positive way. For that to happen, you must trust your destiny.

You can learn to do this, though. Here are three immediate, uncomplicated mindsets to help you convert your thoughts to purposeful thinking:

- You can say that everything you do has purpose.
- You can re-imagine what has happened and show its higher purpose.
- You can create energy just by perceiving that something has a purpose.

Here is an example of purposeful thinking. Let's say that you work at a job you hate. You get up every morning, look in the mirror and say, "I hate my job." Your focus is on what you don't want instead of what you do want.

The way to empower yourself is by accepting your current choice of employment. Think about how the money you are earning is paying for what you need today and believe that there is something better for you out there and you will find it.

Not only will you be excited about your day and your future, but also people will notice you. Life loves happy and excited people, and like attracts like. Even if you can't leave your job immediately, at least you are creating the energy and motivation to do something about it.

Begin today implementing your ability to view everything that happens to you in your life as having a purpose. Fight your urge to return to believing that what you think doesn't matter, develop the habit of purposeful thinking, and know that you are succeeding at finding your purpose.

Step 2: Purposeful Choosing

Purposeful choosing means that you become aware of your choices relative to creating energy. Choose to accept the fact that your life does not include any activities that you find personally satisfying, and choose to include meaningful activities in your life.

Purposeful choosing is not as difficult to do as purposeful thinking. The only way it can work for you, though, is that you must believe you have choices to change your situation and that you are not stuck with the way things are.

It is what you are choosing to include in your day that either creates energy or not. When you constantly engage in activities that you feel no connection to, it decreases your energy. However, when you engage in activities that you do feel a connection to, it increases your energy.

To help you understand, I have created and named these two energies. They are "Circle of Energy" and "Lack of Energy." Circle of Energy symbolizes energy that moves, changes, and flows in a circle. Lack of Energy symbolizes energy that lacks movement, needs constant replacement, and eventually gets stuck.

Lack of Energy got its name because the energy flows just like the letter L. The energy comes in from the top, falls straight down, and then it gets kicked out. It becomes a constant struggle to find energy, keep energy, and then make more energy.

This happens when you are constantly working and doing for others and you neglect to do something that has deep meaning for you. At the end of the day you end up feeling drained, stuck, and stressed out.

Here is one simple way to implement purposeful choosing. Let's say you are at work and a coworker approaches you and asks if you would be available to help plan an annual company party. Before you say yes, remember your two choices. If you are choosing to do more activities in your life that have personal meaning to you and that is not one of them, say no. Remember, when you constantly say yes to other people and no to yourself, you end up stressed and stuck.

Now that you've learned about the two energies, Circle of Energy or Lack of Energy, it is time to show you how to take action to go after your life's purpose and step 3 will show you how to do that.

Step 3: Purposeful Doing

Purposeful doing means that you do an activity that has meaning to you, you feel good about accomplishing it, your energy goes up, and you become energized and motivated to do more.

The power behind this step is that you will go from asking, "What is my life's purpose?" to "What can I do today that has meaning to me?" This makes the process of finding your life's purpose more manageable and empowering.

The challenge to Purposeful Doing is being able to identify which activities would be personally satisfying to you and finding the time to add those meaningful activities to your already busy schedule. Sounds easy, right? It is not easy to do if you are not connected to who you are, if you do not know what you want, or if you lack time and energy.

The best way to meet this challenge is to do a personal satisfaction activity. An activity that is personally satisfying is an activity that you feel personally connected to. On your "My Life Today" sheet in your workbook, the "I want to do" column lists those activities. Feel free to spend more time on this list if you need to. You can add or delete whatever you want.

Now I want you to create a "Purpose and Passion" page in your workbook, as illustrated in the following example. You can photocopy the appropriate page in the appendix of this book and insert it into your workbook.

My Purpose and Passion

Date it	Choose it	Do it	Feel it
3/22	*Journal*	*10 minutes*	*I am energized*

I'm accomplishing my goal!

Go back to your "I want to do" list and pick one activity you are willing to commit to doing. I recommend you pick an activity that is achievable. In the beginning, the important thing is not which activity you pick, what matters most is that you do it. Pick something you really want to do, not something you have to do.

For instance, let's say you really want to journal, but don't feel you have the time or energy to include that in your already busy schedule. Make the decision that you are going to journal first thing in the morning. Place your journal, pen, and a bottle of water on your nightstand the night before. Set your alarm to go off ten minutes earlier than you usually wake up. When your alarm goes off, grab your journal and pen and write for ten minutes.

Now, go get ready for work as usual. Before you go to work, though, go to your "Purpose and Passion" sheet in your workbook and record the date, what you did, and for how long. Follow that with one or two positive affirmations stating something positive about your accomplishment. An example would be, "I am accomplishing my goal of journaling."

The total time to carry out this new strategy is about fifteen minutes: three minutes to get the nightstand ready the night before, ten minutes to journal, and two minutes to write an entry in your workbook. Hopefully, your schedule has room for you to add a fifteen-minute activity. Don't laugh; I meet lots of people who do not have a moment to spare.

For every choice you take and every entry you make, your workbook will become a great source of inspiration for you because it will serve as a record and reminder of all the activities you are choosing to do to live a purposeful life.

I am hoping you resonate with this information, find it easy to use, and immediately notice more energy. My goal is for you to get so good at using this method for everyday stuff that eventually you will use it for deep, life-changing stuff.

You might have read this chapter and decided this information won't help you because your life situation is the way it is and it isn't going to change anytime soon. You probably would love to find your life's purpose, but you are stressed-out, living paycheck-to-paycheck, and unable to balance work and family life, so you figure why try.

The truth is you are right about the fact that right now in your life you lack time, energy, and resources—and your situation is going to continue this way for some time to come. But don't give up! Feeling hopeless will squash every ounce of happiness and joy right out of you. And what affects you, affects your family and loved ones.

As I say many times throughout this book, never give up because it is never too late to go for your dreams. Get up tomorrow knowing you are about to begin living a purposeful life.

Sandra's Success Secrets

You get what you believe you deserve.

Your purpose in life keeps you on your path.

*You must have a purpose for
getting up in the morning.*

3

Uncover Obstacles

𝒞hange is about choice and the choices you make everyday are either moving you forward or holding you back from what you want. You have heard it said many times that you have the choice to accept the things you can't change and change the things you can. That is what this chapter is all about.

To help you get started, you will need to spend some time thinking about and uncovering what you want to change in your life, and then create a motivating reason for making the change. To accomplish this, take the following steps:

1. Identify what is holding you back.

2. Change the thoughts, beliefs, and attitudes that are holding you back.

3. Accept those things you cannot change, and focus on what you can control.

If you find this chapter hard to do, you are not alone. Most successful people will tell you their lives did not change for the better until they saw what was holding them back, chose to do things differently, and accepted the things they just had to live with. My own story serves as a good example. I wanted to change my belief that I was a failure. My good reason to change this belief was because I wanted to write this book. By choosing to see myself as successful, and then developing good writing habits, I wrote this book. I accepted the fact that I did not enjoy writing but I stayed focused on the thought that this book might help you.

Now it is your turn. Grab your workbook and create a page called "My Future Life If Nothing Changes." (You may photocopy the appropriate page from the appendix of this book.) The following eight questions ask you to think about what you and your life will be like in the future if your current thoughts, beliefs, and habits stay the same.

My Future Life If Nothing Changes

1. Who will I become in five years if I stay the same?

2. Where will I be working in five years if things stay the same?

3. How much money will I be earning in five years if things stay the same?

4. Where will I be living in five years if things stay the same?

5. Who will I be In love with in five years if things stay the same?

6. What will I be like in five years if things stay the same?

7. What will I look like in five years if things stay the same?

8. What do I think I won't be doing in five years but wish I were?

Now that you looked at the future, let's look at the present. Make the "My Present Life" page for your workbook (see the appendix for the appropriate page you can photocopy), and answer the following four questions.

My Present Life

1. What negative thoughts, beliefs, and habits are keeping me from my ideal life?

2. Which of those am I able to change?

3. Which of those am I unable to change?

4. Which thoughts, beliefs, and attitudes can I accept that I cannot control or change?

These last three questions will lead you to what exactly it is you need to change and why. This will be your "My Commitment to Change" page, and you will find a page in the appendix that you can photocopy and fill out for your workbook.

My Commitment to Change

1. What do you want to change?

2. What is your reason to change?

3. How are you going to do that?

I am sure you have done this before, but if you haven't, now is the time to decide what you want your future to be like if you could get what you really wanted. Even if you are not sure, write something in. Think big and dream big. Name this page "My Awesome Life in Five Years."

My Awesome Life in Five Years

1. Who will I become in five years?

2. Where will I be working in five years?

3. How much money will I be earning in five years?

4. Where will I be living in five years?

5. Who will I be in love with in five years?

6. What will I be like in five years?

7. What will I look like in five years?

8. What will I be doing in five years that I am most proud of?

9. When will I start creating my new future?

10. How will I begin creating my new future?

The benefit of doing the work in this chapter is that you will discover how your behavior and habits are affected by your thoughts, beliefs, and attitude. Remember, change is about choices. Focus on your everyday choices to get what you really want and live the life you were meant to live.

Sandra's Success Secrets

What you put thought to grows.

Everything you do today affects your tomorrow.

Change the self-beliefs that are holding you back.

4

=== **HOW TO** ===

Embrace Change

*I*f you are serious about getting what you really want in life, chances are you will need to create change in your life. Well, be prepared—change feels funky.

This chapter will show you how to get comfortable outside your comfort zone, uncover what needs to change, and consciously choose new behaviors to enable you to create the personal change necessary to go after and succeed at accomplishing your goals and fulfilling your dreams.

Personal change is when you examine your own thoughts, feelings, and beliefs and choose to change a behavior, habit, or attitude to move you toward a goal or dream. Many people don't realize they can successfully create personal change because they either resist change or try to change things they can't control.

To begin with, people are creatures of habit. You get up in the morning and do the same routine to get ready for work, drive the same route to work, conduct your day the same, drive home the same way, and end the day the same.

But not everyone handles change the same way. Some people are highly adaptable to change, and in fact they need challenge and variety. Others have difficulty adapting to change, and they need control and security.

I am both highly adaptable and I have difficulty adapting to change. As an adaptable person, I love to problem-solve the many challenges of running my own business. I like variety because it makes me feel creative and alive.

Where I have difficulty adapting to change is when it comes to control. I need to be in control because I value freedom and individualism. I need freedom to do what I want, when I want, and in my own way, which offers me the security of knowing that I can depend on myself to create the life I was meant to live.

What about you? Do you need challenge and variety or do you need control and security? Create a "My Needs" page in your workbook. (You may photocopy and use the appropriate page in the appendix of this book.) Write down things you do, or that you would like to do, and ask yourself if that activity meets your need for challenge, variety, control, or security.

If, after looking at the page, you realize your needs aren't being met, it might be time to do something different.

My Needs				
What I do	Challenge	Variety	Control	Security
(Write in activity)	*(Check which need applies)*			

I believe that all four needs are important regardless if you are highly adaptable or not. Where you run into trouble is when you become overly focused on one particular need. For instance, being extremely security-driven can keep you from challenging yourself to try something new. To put it another way, you create balance by avoiding extremes.

Let's review what you just learned:

- Create personal change to change your life.

- Get comfortable outside your comfort zone.

- Uncover what needs to change, and then choose new behaviors.

- Create balance by avoiding extremes.

Now it is time to make change happen. I have created three solutions that will help you accomplish personal change. You will probably find this difficult to do at first, but keep at it until it becomes second nature. Here are the three solutions:

1. Accept your fear.

2. Challenge your beliefs.

3. Decide to change.

Solution #1: Accept Your Fear

The best information I found that helped me deal with my own inability to change was when I was trying to lose weight. I came across the book *Different Bodies, Different Diets* by Dr. Carolyn L. Mein. This book is not about change; it is about diets. The author created a whole system of body types and a diet to fit each body type.

In this book I read how change triggers old fears and feelings of inadequacy and we will avoid those feelings at all cost. Bingo. That was so true for me! Every time I tried to change, I immediately felt fearful and inadequate so I would quickly retreat back to my comfort zone.

Today, when I step out of my comfort zone and I feel funky, I continue with my goal until the negative feeling fades. As a result of my courage, I have accomplished more than I ever could have imagined.

Change the response pattern you're locked into. Do something new, feel funky, and stay with that negative feeling until it fades. Eventually, you will find yourself outside your comfort zone accomplishing things you never thought possible. Guaranteed!

Solution #2: Challenge Your Beliefs

Your core beliefs have a huge influence on how you experience your life and they have a tremendous impact on how you approach change. Core beliefs speak to what you believe about yourself and what you expect of yourself.

Sadly, for many of us our core beliefs aren't our own. They are judgments we heard from others and we have adopted them as our own. There are six basic core beliefs:

1. **Self-worth: How do you feel about yourself?**

2. **Self-expectations: What do you expect of yourself?**

3. **Change tolerance: Can you tolerate the uneasy feeling change evokes?**

4. **Abilities: Do you have the skills and abilities to go after what you want?**

5. **Self-esteem: Do you believe you deserve what it is you want?**

6. **Self-determination: Do you take responsibility for your own life?**

Investigate your core beliefs by answering yes or no to the following questions. There is a copy of this questionnaire in the appendix of this book that you can photocopy and fill out for your workbook.

Core Belief Questionnaire

Yes No

___ ___ Do you believe you're *worthy* of success?

___ ___ Do you *expect* to have a great life?

___ ___ Do you believe you can *change?*

___ ___ Do you believe you have *what it takes* to succeed?

___ ___ Do you believe you *deserve* what you want?

___ ___ Do you believe you are *responsible* for your own life?

If you answered no on the core belief questionnaire, you have succeeded at the first step required for change—you have become aware of a belief that might be holding you back. The second step is to develop positive core beliefs that empower you to get what you really want.

How do you develop positive core beliefs? You start by taking responsibility for your life by believing and expecting much of yourself. Do it every day for everything until it becomes habit. If you need more help, refer back to chapters one and two.

When you can say yes to all the core beliefs listed in the above questionnaire, you will be unstoppable.

Solution #3: Decide to Change

I remember attending a speaker's conference, and motivational speaker Les Brown was the keynote speaker. He told a great story about how an airline gate agent upgraded him to first class. When asked why he did that the gate agent replied, "Because I can."

Sometimes we can decide to do something different for nothing more than "Because we can." Decide today that you will change your thinking. Decide today that you will not settle for living a half-lived life. Decide today that you will find your authentic self.

I know this third remedy sounds too simple to be true; but believe me when I say that the simple act of making up your mind to do something is powerful. Once you begin doing all the things you thought you'd never do and someone stops and asks you why you decided to change jobs, or start a business, or travel to Europe, just look at them and say, "Because I can." Enough said.

I want to end this chapter by going back and reexamining something I wrote earlier. Remember in Solution #1, "Accept Your Fear," I talked about your response pattern? This is a concept I developed to help you identify what occurs when you think or feel something. What you do is called your response. In other words, a response pattern is how you automatically respond to the events in your life.

A negative response pattern will move you away from what it is you want and a positive response pattern will move you toward what you want. Which way do you want to go?

How do you go from a negative response pattern to a positive response pattern? Use what I have already taught you and make a conscious choice to:

- Feel the fear and do it anyway.
- Challenge a negative core belief.
- Just make up your mind that you can.

Change isn't the challenge, it's getting beyond the funky feeling change evokes that is the challenge. If you can get beyond that funky feeling, you can get what you really want and live the life of your dreams.

Sandra's Success Secrets

You can't change what you can't see.

Change triggers fears and what you fear you resist.

Embrace change to get what you really want in life.

5

Improve Communication

*I*n order for you to improve communication, connect with people, and create success, you must lay this foundation:

- Possess a strong sense of self.

- Communicate well.

- Value relationships.

Internal Communication

Before we discuss how to communicate with others, let's discuss internal communication. Here is a fact: What you consistently say and feel about yourself internally can either strengthen or weaken your sense of self, and that affects how you relate to others.

Your Inner Self-Talk

A couple of years ago, Oprah did a show on the benefits of journaling. I loved the ideas that were presented, so I went to a bookstore, bought a beautiful leather journal, and wrote my first entry that night.

For the next three months I recorded my thoughts, feelings, and goals. Then one day I just stopped writing. To tell you the truth, I didn't like journaling because I thought it was a waste of my time. I stuck my journal away in a drawer and decided that was the end of that.

About six months later, while cleaning out my bedroom, I came across my leather journal. That evening, I made myself a cup of hot tea and read every page I had written six months earlier. What I read shocked me. No, I was horrified.

The first week of entries talked about how happy and excited I was about a new business idea I was pursuing. I wrote about how motivated I felt when I got up in the morning, what tasks I had accomplished during the day, and how proud of myself I felt at the end of the day.

As I continued reading though I realized that all the entries after the first week changed from positive to downright degrading. Here are a few excerpts: "You are so stupid." "Who do you think you are?" "You will never make it." This went on entry after entry, page after page.

I made an important self-discovery that evening: my inner self-talk was negative. The sad part was that I wasn't even aware of the fact that I was saying unkind, mean words to myself until I read it in my journal. No wonder I couldn't succeed.

Your Inner Critic

Then I made another self-discovery: I had internalized the unkind words my dad had spoken to me as a child, and when I grew up I spoke those same unkind words to myself because I continued to believe that what he said to me was not only important but also correct.

That voice that speaks negative criticism to you in your head is called your inner critic. The job of your inner critic is to keep you safe and acceptable to others by criticizing yourself before other people criticize you.

Reading my journal that evening showed me how every time I tried to change, pursue a goal, or achieve a dream my inner critic would criticize me in an effort to keep me safe and from failing. I had become my own worse critic.

Many times while writing this book I would hear my inner critic say, "You will never write a book worth reading." Yikes! Can you see how difficult it would be for me to finish my book if I didn't believe it was going to be of value to anyone?

If you feel stuck and believe your inner critic may be the culprit, you may want to do this next exercise. Your workbook should have a section for this chapter, and your first page in this section will be titled "My Inner Critic" (see the appendix for the page to photocopy for this purpose). Please answer these questions as well as you can.

Communication: My Inner Critic

1. Do you feel you have an inner critic?

2. If you answered yes, what does it say to you?

3. Does it get worse under certain conditions?

4. What are those conditions?

5. When you listen to your inner critic, whose voice are you hearing?

6. When you decide to change or accomplish something outside of your comfort zone, what does your inner critic say?

7. Are you hearing positive or negative comments?

8. Does your inner critic keep you stuck?

If you found those questions difficult to answer, you are not alone because dealing with the fact that you have an inner critic is no small feat. Once you become aware of it, however, there are things you can do to lessen its negative effect.

Here are three ideas you can implement immediately to deal with your inner critic:

1. Recognize when it's speaking.

2. Realize it is not who you are; it is just a part of you.

3. Reduce its power by speaking back to it.

This is how to make this work. Let's say one day you decide you want to lose weight. You commit to a healthy diet and exercise. The first week is a breeze. Then, something changes. You begin to notice that when you are walking you are saying to yourself, "Walking won't help me because I can't lose weight."

Believe me, an empowered individual does not speak those words when he or she needs motivation. Train yourself to recognize when your inner critic is speaking. Realize that your inner critic is a part of you, but it is not you. Get the courage to speak back to your inner critic by saying, "I will succeed at walking because I will keep walking."

Remember, your inner critic is powerful enough to make you give up a dream and it is going to criticize you until you do give up in hopes that it will save you from potential failure. Don't let it; override its voice with your empowered voice to go after and get what you really want in life.

A final note about journaling: I have learned to love journaling and I recommend it highly. It is the best way to flesh out on paper everything that is floating around in your head. It serves as a guidebook of where you want to go, where you have been, and all of the changes in between.

Your Inner Strength

When you have an encounter with a crabby, unhappy person and you are totally unaffected by the person's poor communication skills and behavior, you have great inner strength. If, on the other hand, they push your button and you end up feeling like a victim, you could use some help creating inner strength. The next section will show you how to do that.

Three Ingredients for Unlimited Inner Strength

1. Know who you are.

2. Embrace the essence of who you are.

3. Fill yourself with lots of self-respect.

The first element, knowing who you are, builds an internal foundation that is solid and unshakeable—just what you need to handle everyday life situations. If you, however, question everything you say and every decision you make, you weaken your ability to speak up, move forward, and grow.

Because it is so important for you to know who you are, I would like you to take some time and dig a little deeper. Think about, discover, and reinforce who you are by creating a "Who Am I" sheet for your workbook. See the appendix for a page to photocopy and use.

What words come to mind when you think of you? Please write them down as in the following example.

Who Am I?

outgoing	*spiritual*	*bold*
direct	*creative*	*thoughtful*
opinionated	*sexy*	*warm*
charismatic	*quiet*	*happy*

Want to know how this information can be useful? Well, if the "Who Am I" sheet lists positive attributes, be sure to include those words in your positive inner self-talk and confidently communicate your true self to others. If you wrote down negative attributes about yourself, choose to communicate positive inner self-talk to yourself until it becomes a habit.

Slowly, your interactions with others will begin to change in a positive way because your self-perception will begin to change in a positive way. Having feelings of high self-worth and a solid sense of who you are equips you to take more risks. It is risky business to break out of your comfort zone to get what you really want.

The second ingredient is that you must always embrace the essence of who you are. Never wish to be like someone else. Becoming a great communicator is not about changing who you are. Communication is about being the real you.

The third and last ingredient for creating inner strength is self-respect. You must be filled with self-respect because when you don't get it, you still have it. In other words, never look outside yourself for something you should give to yourself.

For example, you might work in an environment where management does not empower, recognize, or reward you for a job well done because either they are horrible managers or they lack the time to connect with their people. If quitting is not an option, go home every day knowing you did an outstanding job.

Some of you work at jobs where you have to deal with rude, mean people. Don't let them push your button; it's not about you. Remember, your self-respect is the best shield to guard against others having the ability to tear you down.

How do you build self-respect? Well, to respect something is to accept it. Simply put, to have self-respect means that you like yourself for who you are, just as you are, with no judgment about how you can or cannot do something. So, self-acceptance is what builds self-respect.

Communicating with Others

Nothing is more important to your success and happiness than your relationships with other people. For that reason, an important skill for you to develop is the ability to recognize other people's communication style and adapt to their style.

I used to be a horrible communicator because I was terribly blunt and overly direct. People usually responded to me one of two ways: either they would become defensive and yell or they would get quiet and run away. It never occurred to me that I sounded mean and condescending. I always figured they were the problem, not me!

Today, I take every opportunity available to meet, listen to, or help someone. I can't tell you how many wonderful conversations and business contacts I have made just waiting in line to order a mocha at Starbuck's.

Remember, in order for you to connect with people and create success, you must have the courage to reach out to someone and see the value of relationships—for they hold the key to your happiness and success!

Your Personality Style

How do you communicate with people? Are you direct, or are you quiet and reserved? Do you like working with other people, or do you prefer to work alone? Do you come across the way you do depending on the circumstances? No matter which way you are, no one way is better than the other.

You are the way you are because early in your life you had a dominant style that became a habit. Much will change in your life, but your style of communicating will be with you all your life.

You are probably familiar with the numerous personality assessment methods available that can help you figure out your personality style. I teach personality styles in many of my seminars and most people find the information very helpful.

After studying numerous models, I took the best of what I learned, combined it with what I learned from working with hundreds of people in my workshops, and came up with an easy-to-understand approach to how to be an effective communicator.

This discussion is based on how others see you, not how you see yourself. In other words, your communication style is determined by other people's perception of two of your behaviors: your level of directness and level of responsiveness.

Your Assertiveness

Let's start with directness. Here are characteristics of someone who would be considered very direct: decisive, quick, and displays lots of energy. In other words, the more decisive, quick, and energetic you appear to be, the more you will be perceived as direct, also known as assertive.

If people see you as less direct, you would be considered not as assertive. Someone who would be perceived as being less direct would appear to have these characteristics: indirect, slow, and less energetic.

On a scale from 1 to 10, 1 being not very direct and 10 being really direct, where would you be?

Not very direct							Really direct
1	2	3	4	5	6	7	8	9	10

Being seen as more assertive or less assertive is based on other people's perception of you. For instance, you might feel excited and gung-ho on the inside but on the outside you display calmness; therefore, the other person could perceive you as not very assertive.

By the same token, you might be very calm inside, but outwardly you jump up and down with arms waving; so the other person could perceive you as more assertive. This is about how people see you behave, not what your true personality is like on the inside.

Your Responsiveness to People

Now let's look at how you respond to people. Here are characteristics of someone who would be perceived as people-oriented: friendly, expressive, likes being with others. So, the more friendly, expressive, and involved with others you appear to be, the more you would be perceived as people-oriented.

If people see that you respond less to others, you could be perceived as task-oriented. Someone who would be perceived as task-oriented would appear to have these characteristics: reserved, structured, and prefers working alone. Sometimes you have strong feelings inside, but choose not to show your feelings on the outside.

On a scale from 1 to 10, 1 being not very responsive to others and 10 being really responsive to others, where would you be?

Not very responsive						Really responsive			
1	2	3	4	5	6	7	8	9	10

How can you use this information? Well, once you know your level of directness and your orientation toward people or tasks, you can choose to slide your dial to the level of the person you are communicating with. You don't change who you are, you simply slide to their range on the scale to lessen your communication differences.

Here is a great analogy. When I write, I sit at my computer for hours. To break up the monotony, I listen to iTunes. One minute I crank up the music and the next minute I can barely hear the song. My volume dial is constantly sliding up and down all day long to suit my needs.

My ability to adjust the volume on my computer is exactly how communication works. You have a certain range you are most comfortable with and you have the ability to adjust your directness and responsiveness levels based on your interactions with others.

Your ability to move outside your comfort level and get in sync with their range is what creates the perception that you get along with them. And remember, the real you is always there.

If after reading about assertiveness and responsiveness you are not sure where you are on the scale, I have provided an exercise to help you figure that out. We do this in my communication workshops and it works pretty well. Copy the corresponding page from the appendix for your workbook, and record your findings.

Exercise to Determine Assertiveness/Responsiveness

Find a partner. This exercise works best if you do not know one another. Share information about yourself for five minutes, then allow your partner to share information about himself or herself for five minutes.

Write down one word to describe how you see yourself and write down one word to describe your partner. Have your partner do the same thing. Don't look at each other's notes.

Compare what you wrote with your partner. For some of you, the words you wrote down will match your partner's words exactly, and for others your words may be totally different. For instance, you may have described your partner as confident and that person wrote down that he or she is insecure.

How Others See Me

"People think I am _____, and I think I am_____."

_____

_____

Using me as an example, I would write: "People think I am demanding, and I think I am determined." They get this impression of me because I can act and sound very direct. I am direct, but only because I have high expectations of myself, I am very focused and driven, and I am determined to fulfill my destiny.

Whether you matched words with your partner is not the point. The point of this exercise is that I want you to realize that how you see yourself can sometimes be different than how others see you. Your partner decided what you are like based on what you said and how you said it.

Remember, too, that communication isn't just about what you say. In fact, only 7 percent of your message is verbal and 93 percent of your message is non-verbal. That is why it is important to be aware of what message you are sending with your body language and tone.

For instance, don't roll your eyes and cross your arms when you are telling someone everything is fine with you. You have to match up what you say with how you look when you say it.

How to Speak Up

It's not always easy to speak up to a rude customer at work or a snippy cashier at the grocery store. Only you can decide if you should speak up and what you should say. But if you need to speak up, speak up even if it feels funky because you are responsible for communicating your needs to people.

There are a couple of good reasons why people don't speak up when they should. Some people try to avoid conflict and confrontation, others were raised with the message that they must get along with others, and some people are just hardwired to be less assertive.

So, how do you speak up? First you must know what you want, then ask for it, and there is a right way to do that. What you don't want to do is always give up your rights or always take away another's rights.

The following is a simple layout, explanation, and example of how to speak up by using "I" statements, being direct, and being quiet. I recommend you take this information and use it as a guide to create your own script.

Use "I" Statements:
Drive the conversation by stating how you feel
rather than you telling others what they are doing wrong.

Good example: "I am concerned about an e-mail I received."

Bad example: "You wrote and sent me a horrible e-mail!"

Be direct:
Get to the point; less is more.
Also, ask for what you do want rather than asking
for what you don't want.

Good example: "I would appreciate it if next time we could discuss the challenges we are having in person."

Bad example: "You left the meeting and walked down to Dave's office and then you sat at his computer and typed up this really mean e-mail message. Then you sent it to everyone in the office, which I think is really tacky."

Be quiet:
Say what you need to say, and then be quiet.
Sometimes silence can make you uncomfortable.
Here's a secret: silence is powerful.

In summary, it is important for you to remember that when it comes to communication, how you communicate with yourself is the most important communication skill you can learn. You must know who you are, know what you want and ask for it, and repeatedly take action over and over again as you pursue your goals.

When it comes to communicating with others, adjusting your dial to their level of assertiveness and responsiveness to lessen your communication differences is an option—you can choose to flex or not flex. Having the skills and the ability to choose to adapt is what makes you good at communication.

Always accept yourself just as you are, develop the skills necessary to effectively communicate with others, and flex when you need to create great relationships. As I always love to say, success is liking yourself, liking what you do, and liking how you do it.

Sandra's Success Secrets

Talk nice to yourself.

Communication starts on the inside.

When it is time to speak up, speak up!

6

Handle Emotions

*T*his chapter will show you how to handle your emotions and take control of your thoughts so you can focus all your positive mental energy on obtaining what you really want—without the guilt.

Dealing with Difficult Situations

Have you ever gotten up in the morning and felt great? You looked in the mirror and loved the way your hair looked . . . You felt like you were losing weight . . . You were full of energy . . . You could conquer the world.

You get in your car and head to work. On the way to work you notice you are making every traffic light. You stop and get a mocha at Starbucks and it tastes just the way you like it.

You pull into the driveway at work, park your car, and grab your coffee. As you get out of your car, you look over and notice the one person you don't want to see—you are looking at a coworker who gets on your nerves. I call this person your poo-poo head.

Well, guess what? Now you are thinking about the one person you don't want to think about, and you are no longer thinking about your wonderful morning. Not only that, but you might think about this person for hours, days, or months no matter how hard you try to get him or her out of your head.

Without the ability to control your thoughts, you can find yourself obsessively replaying conversations and events over and over in your mind, which can keep you focused on what you don't want to think about rather than what you do want to think about.

If that sounds like you, it is time to take control of your thoughts. The way to begin this discussion is to think about what you can and cannot control. There is a connection between taking control of your thoughts and knowing what you can and cannot control.

Go to the section for this chapter in your workbook and photocopy the "Things I Can't Control/My Stressors" page. Now, let's look at all the things you think you can't control. Your list might include your workload, negative people, or lack of time. Another way to look at this is to list everything you consider to be stressful to you. Go ahead and list your stressors.

Things I Can't Control/My Stressors

_____

_____

_____

_____

_____

_____

_____

Now, photocopy the "Things I Can Control" page for your workbook, and list all the things you think you can control. Your list might include your attitude, your behavior, or your choices.

Things I Can Control

_____

_____

_____

_____

_____

_____

_____

Here is what I want you to realize from these two lists: The more you focus on what you can't control, the worse it gets. The more you focus on what you can control, the less the things you can't control—your stressors—bother you.

What that means is that if you are upset and you focus on the problem, the problem gets worse. But the minute you choose to not take it personally, and think about what you can do to deal with the situation, you can come up with a solution.

So, what is the one thing you can control when faced with a negative person or situation? The answer is that you can control your response. I know you have heard it said before that it is not what happens to you that matters, it's your response to what happens to you that matters.

The solution to dealing with a difficult person or situation is to remember you always have three choices. I will explain each choice and help you find a way to use these three choices every day in every situation so that you never feel victimized by someone else again.

When dealing with a difficult person or situation, these are your three choices:

> **1. Accept it: "Whatever"**
>
> **2. Change it: "Speak up"**
>
> **3. Leave it: "Move on"**

Choice #1: Accept It

The first choice is to accept it. What does that mean? Well, that means you take responsibility for all your choices by accepting the things you can't change and changing the things you can.

Here is an example of what happened to me and how I chose a response. One day I was speaking at a business conference for about 150 women. During the morning break, a woman attending the conference walked up to me and said, "Sandra, I need to tell you something. You suck. You are a horrible speaker."

At the end of the conference another woman walked up to me and said, "Can I talk with you?" I am thinking, *Great here we go again, another unhappy person.* She said, "Sandra, it's me, Lea."

The only Lea I knew was a petite woman with long blonde hair. This woman was completely bald, no eyelashes, and no eyebrows. Her cheeks were puffy and the whites of her eyes were yellow.

I said, "I'm sorry, I don't think we know one another." She said, "Yes, Sandra, I have heard you speak numerous times. You just don't recognize me because my chemo and radiation treatments make me look like I do. I was diagnosed with breast cancer about six months ago."

She continued, "About three months ago, I heard you were going to be speaking so I bought a ticket to see you. After I bought my ticket, I realized my cancer treatment was on the same day as your event. Yesterday, a nurse phoned to say they had to reschedule my treatment for tomorrow."

By now I am frozen. She continued softly, "Before I go I want to tell you something. The worst thing that has happened to me is getting this diagnosis. The best thing that has happened to me since getting diagnosed is spending this day with you. I believe things happen for a reason and I am just so thankful that I got to see you. Your words will strengthen me as I fight this cancer. Sandra, you're awesome."

As I looked into her eyes, I realized the importance of that moment because I knew there was a chance I would be seeing her for the last time. As she walked away, we promised each other that we would stay in touch. We have stayed in touch, and I am happy to report that she is recovering and life is slowly returning to normal for her.

Getting back to that day at the conference: In the morning a woman told me I sucked and in the afternoon a woman told me I was awesome. What do you think I said to the woman who said I sucked?

After she said, "You suck," I paused for a moment and then said, "Thank you." Then, with a blank look on my face, I looked at her a moment longer, then walked away. I made the choice to accept the fact that she did not like me.

Do you want know what I said to myself? Inside I said, "WHATEVER!" When I teach this to people at my seminars, I have them throw their hands up into the air, make an ugly look on their face, and yell out, "WHATEVER!" It's what I call doing the ugly.

Of course, you don't really need to do all that stuff, but inside, saying "WHATEVER!" to yourself is a way for you to respond, rather than react. It means you are choosing not to become emotional with a negative person. And negative people just hate it when you don't react.

To stay silent and say nothing to someone does not mean you accept his or her bad behavior or negativity; it just means you choose not to get emotional by choosing not to speak up. And, silence is powerful.

Choice #2: Change It

Change it is the second choice. What does that mean? Change it does not mean you must change or that you must change the person you are dealing with. Change it means that you must speak up when you are dealing with a situation that is no longer acceptable.

To speak up means to assert yourself. To assert yourself is to speak up on your own behalf, which can be difficult to do at times. It is important to remember, though, that it is your responsibility to say something to someone who has overstepped his or her boundary with you.

In chapter five, "How to Improve Communication," you learned the right way to speak up. So, for this discussion on being assertive and speaking up, it is the same script:

- **Ask for what you want.**

- **Use "I" language expressing a comment about yourself, rather than a "you" message that puts the other person on the defensive.**

- **Be direct, to the point, and then be quiet.**

As with any new skill, you must prepare and practice it ahead of time so that when you actually need to deliver the message, you are ready. I suggest you take a moment and think about your poo-poo head, think about what he or she typically says to you that pushes your button, then create a response to say the next time it happens.

Here is an example that might help you. Let's say a coworker has a habit of going through your desk while you are at lunch. You know this to be true because when you return from lunch, your breath mints are gone and they have the freshest breath in the office! Copy the appendix page titled "Assertiveness Script," and insert it into this chapter of your workbook. Then write your own script. It could sound like the following script:

Assertiveness Script

Linda, when I returned from lunch, I realized my breath mints were gone.

I consider my desk to be my personal space.

I would appreciate it if you would ask me if you need anything, and I will get it for you before I go to lunch.

Only you can decide if you need to assert yourself or not. If you don't think you should say something, then don't. If you think you need to say something, speak up. You are responsible for all of your communication decisions.

Choice #3: Leave It

The third choice is to leave it. What does that mean? It means you need to move on. That can be taken figuratively or literally. You can move on emotionally or you can move physically. You decide. But when it is time to move on, get the courage to do it.

I believe that when you are unable to let go of people, things, or emotions that are no longer serving you, it creates stress. Eventually, all the negative stuff you are carrying around with you can topple you over.

In my own life, I had a migraine so painful that I ended up in the emergency room. I cracked a back tooth from biting too hard. I used to be overweight because I overate. All of those problems were caused from stress.

Be an attentive guardian of your own mental, emotional, physical, and spiritual health. If you feel your stress building, it might be time to let go of something. Take immediate action before it is too late.

If You Can't Stop Reacting

This is an exercise you can do when you are in the middle of an emotional or difficult situation. I created this idea of two zones and I call it "Moving from your heart zone to your head zone." It will take time for you to get the hang of it, but once you do, I think you will find it helpful.

Exercise:
Moving from Your Heart Zone to Your Head Zone

Think of your heart zone as the area that deals with feelings and emotions. Think of your head zone as the area that deals with problem solving and solutions.

Right now, I want you to think about a person you would consider your poo-poo head. It can be a supervisor, a coworker, or maybe a neighbor. Did you feel a change inside you? Does it feel like a negative feeling or emotion?

This is what I call being in your heart zone with an itchy feeling. It is important for you to always acknowledge your feelings when you are in your heart zone. Ignoring your feelings will not make them go away.

The problem with staying in your heart zone is that it is almost impossible to figure out a solution when you are focused on the itchy feeling. You need to redirect your thinking to something positive.

The way to handle your emotions and control your thinking is to move up to your head zone. Once you are there, ask yourself, "Is this something I can control?" If the answer is yes, try it. If the answer is no, ask yourself, "What is it that I *can* control?" The answer is: You can control your response.

I want you to pick your response. Say to yourself, "Now that this person has done something that has upset me, I can accept it, change it, or leave it." I want to you to pick one. If you are feeling particularly emotional and unable to pick one, try the same process again in about fifteen minutes.

Here is an example of how to pick a response. Let's say you recently received a promotion and a coworker is jealous of you. You overheard this person talking about how she felt you didn't deserve to be promoted. Let's look at your choices.

Accept it: You would say to *yourself*, "I accept the fact that she is jealous of my promotion and I will ignore her rudeness."

Change it: You would say to your jealous *coworker*, "I understand you were talking to Brenda about my promotion. I would appreciate it if you would talk to me personally if you have any comments."

Leave it: You would move on from the experience. Moving on can be taken figuratively or literally: move on in your mind or move on and get a new job.

You have the choice to redirect your thinking, but only if you feel you have power to do so. It's when others are allowed to get inside your head and you can't get them out that you lose your power.

The Power of Acceptance

I want to talk about the power of accepting the things you cannot change and changing the things you can. Here are three acceptance principles, along with an explanation of what they mean.

Acceptance Principle #1

Two percent of everyone you meet will not like you.

Explanation: No matter how much you try, no matter how much you care, no matter how thoughtful you are, two percent of everyone you meet will not like you. If you expect everyone to like you and you get hurt when they don't, I recommend you embrace this 2% principle.

Some days an audience doesn't like me, other days they do.

Either way, I always accept the fact that not everyone is going to like me. In other words, I never allow their opinion of me to throw me off my path to my destiny.

Acceptance Principle #2
He or she who angers you controls you.

Explanation: When someone finds your emotional button, they will push it! And, if you allow it to continue, they will push it over and over. The best way to cover your emotional button is to learn how to respond, not react—and that is what this chapter is all about.

Acceptance Principle #3
"It's not about me."

Explanation: When you see someone's facial expression, or think you hear a tone change, or watch someone's body language and assess that it's about you, it probably is not. And if it is about you, remember: "WHATEVER!"

You must always feel good about yourself regardless if someone likes you or not. Stay focused on what you can control. You cannot control another person's opinion of you, but you can choose to decide it's not about you.

The good news is that when you embrace the concept that everything is not about you, the easier it will be not to take everything personally. Now you can control your thoughts, choose your focus, and find a solution.

Quick Way to Retain Emotional Control

You can always head for the ALPS when you must deal with a negative person or situation:

Acknowledge your feelings.

Leave your "feeling zone" and go up to your "thinking zone."

Pick one of your three choices: accept, change, or leave it.

Stay focused on the solution and forget about the poo-poo head.

Read this chapter as many times as it takes to learn how to handle your emotions. Let go of any guilt you have about speaking up for yourself. And vow to keep your heart zone and head zone full of positive, empowering thoughts.

Sandra's Success Secrets

You always get to choose your focus.

He or she who angers you, controls you.

Always cover your emotional button.

7

———— **HOW TO** ————

Face Fear

ear has the power to stop you in your tracks. Fear can keep you locked in a cycle of failure by forcing you to continually relive your negative experiences. Worst of all, fear can keep you from living the life you were meant to live.

I used to worry about everything. I worried that I would be a horrible mother, that I would never meet a wonderful man, and that I would have to work at a job I hated just to pay the bills. I was so mentally stuck on worry and fear that I felt unable to make better choices that could have helped me change my life for the better.

What Do You Fear?

So, what do you fear? Do you worry a lot? Do you feel vulnerable? Do you feel like something bad is going to happen? Go to this chapter's section in your workbook, and insert a photocopy of the matching page from the appendix. Begin by listing everything you fear—whether real or imagined.

What Do I Fear?

_____

_____

_____

Uncovering your fears and then recognizing if you are fear-based or not can help you tackle your obstacles. Fear-based thinking focuses you on the worst-case scenario. Empowered-based thinking acknowledges your emotions, and then devises a solution.

There are two universal fears that can keep you stuck: fear of failure and fear of success. You have probably read about these two fears, but it's worth remembering how debilitating they can be.

Universal Fear #1: Fear of Failure

Fear of failure is about fearing the worst in you. Rationally, your fear is unfounded because your fear is imagined. Fear is an emotion that exists when you don't have the trust that you can do what it is you want to do.

If you fear failure, you can find it unimaginable to believe you will succeed at accomplishing something. Just the thought of failing can keep you stuck in the "not doing." When you finally attempt to do something new and you give up at the first sign you might fail, you don't fully give yourself a chance to succeed.

If you have an opportunity to read about people who have succeeded at accomplishing something great, you will find out that they failed many times before succeeding. It was their determination and their not giving up that created their success.

Universal Fear #2: Fear of Success

Can you imagine fearing success? I think of all fears, this one takes the cake for being the weirdest. Who wouldn't want to set goals and achieve them? Why would you fear succeeding? Who wouldn't want success?

We all have a window of belief. In that window of belief sits what we feel about ourselves. If we believe we will never have what it is we're going after, we will not have it. We must feel worthy of success or we will sabotage our success every time. Let me explain.

In the past, I had a deep desire to be successful at owning my own business. I would set up a business, then fail. During the process I could see that I was doing things in a manner that was not successful. I was intelligent enough to know what I was doing was ineffective, but I was unable to make myself go about it in a more successful way.

On a deep level, I needed to prove myself right that I did not deserve success so I helped myself fail. This is called self-sabotage. If you remember that I feared failure, too, you can see that I had fear at both ends. I feared I would fail before I even began, and feared succeeding once I got started.

Internal Emotional Blocks

Now I want to talk about internal emotional blocks to success that are fear-driven. I will also give you tips and strategies on how to overcome them. See if you identify with any of these.

Shame

Shame is defined as feeling unworthy. When you feel not acceptable just as you are, it creates shame. This feeling of not being acceptable, worthy, or capable can undermine your sense of self.

If you are blocked by fear before taking action, shame might be the culprit. What negative core beliefs are you hanging on to from childhood that are lowering your self-worth and creating shame?

Do you have memories of statements the important people in your life said to you when you were young? Here is an example, "Shame on you! Who do you think you are!"

What you can do about it: Because your self-perceptions and beliefs are distorted by the fear that something is wrong with you, let's look at what your negative core beliefs have you believing. In others words, what do you falsely believe yourself to be?

Go back to the appendix and copy the page titled "My Negative Labels" for your workbook. To use me as an example, I used to label myself lazy, stupid, and unfocused. I want you to take your time to think about and record all of the labels you have inherited from others or you created yourself.

My Negative Labels

I tell myself that I am:

lazy _____

stupid _____

unfocused _____

Since self-worth is the opposite of shame, what can you begin believing about yourself? Please rewrite the above negative labels to positive messages. Once you rewrite them, I encourage you to consciously think these thoughts over and over until they become who you are.

Always remember that personal power is knowing that you matter, accepting yourself just as you are, and refusing to be a victim. Feeling empowered builds the structure for personal growth.

Now I want you to rewrite your negative labels to something positive—whether you believe them to be true or not. Do this on a photocopied page from the appendix titled "My Positive Labels" and insert it into your workbook. It is important to shed negative labels that no longer serve you. My positive self-talk rewrites from above are creative, smart, and focused, which are inserted into the example.

My Positive Labels

I am:

creative _____

smart _____

focused _____

In a previous chapter, you read about the difference between self-esteem and self-respect. Self-respect means total self-acceptance unconditionally. That means you accept yourself whether you can or cannot do something.

Get passionate about loving your true self. If you don't know who you really are, begin to learn today by listening to your inner voice that speaks your truth. Never wish to be like anyone else. And, remove old labels that no longer fit you.

Others' Disapproval

When you live in fear of disapproval from others, you place them in a position where they can either raise or lower your sense of self based on their interaction with you. Your decisions are made to please them, and not necessarily to do what is best for you.

When you value their opinion of you more than you value your own, you will err on the side of quieting your voice by holding back your feelings and opinions. Because the goal is not to make anyone angry and to be liked, you always play it safe and stay in your comfort zone.

What you can do about it: Your goal is to be less and less dependent on the good opinion of others in order to feel good about yourself. Dr. Wayne Dyer calls this being a self-actualizing person. When you do something either it works or it doesn't work, but your sense of self is not dependent on other people's assessment of your accomplishment.

Another remedy: you can start speaking up. Sometimes your fear of speaking up can block communication and that can lead to disaster. As much as you want to avoid conflict and confrontation, your ability to communicate is imperative to your success.

The method of how to speak up is similar to the information in chapter five. In this communication message you take responsibility for your own emotions by speaking up without blaming the other person.

Here is the speaking-up technique:

A Tell them what happened without blame.

B Tell them how you feel.

C Tell them how it affects or concerns you.

The following script is the standard approach to the Speaking-Up Technique. You can use this as a script, or blueprint, for the next time you need to speak up. Speak about the problem without blaming the other person, state how you feel, and inform the person of possible consequences.

A   *When we talk about your mother . . .*
B   *I feel frustrated . . .*
C   *Because I am put in the middle of a difficult situation.*

Here's another example:

A   *When the meeting deviates from the agenda . . .*
B   *I am concerned . . .*
C   *Because not everyone has enough time to present their ideas.*

Wanting to Be Perfect

The fear of making a mistake is a learned response that comes from making a mistake in the past. In other words, you're reliving the past. If every time you begin something and you feel you will make a mistake, you relive something that has already happened.

What you can do about it: You are not allowing what should happen in the present to happen but rather superimposing a past image into the present. Be aware of this and stop doing it. Give yourself a chance to see how things turn out. Just because you made a mistake in the past doesn't necessarily mean you will make the same mistake again.

To this day, if I am ever asked to make pie crust my reply is, "I can't." If you ask me why, I will tell you it's because I flunked the pie crust final exam in my eighth grade home economics class!

Guilt

Guilt makes you feel as though you did something wrong. When you attach your doing something wrong to the failure of something, you can end up feeling guilty. Fear of failure drives guilt. Ongoing guilt erodes your sense of self-worth.

For some women, feelings of guilt arise when they do something just for themselves, and that can feel as though they are doing something wrong. Always doing for others feels like such a wonderful, selfless act, but doing something just for you can feel selfish.

What you can do about it: Guilt is used as a powerful tool to control others. When others try to use it on you, you must be strong and speak up. They want you to feel as though the problem or the mistake was your "fault." You are not responsible for others' failures.

If you allow guilt to grow, it will chop away at your sense of self, piece by piece. Guard against this by not accepting responsibility for other people's emotions and for mistakes you did not make. Again, speak up.

You must stop feeling guilty when you do something just for you. You are responsible for taking care of your personal needs in order to be fully present to those around you. It is important to regularly renew, refresh, and replenish your personal energy. Stop depleting yourself!

How to Face and Conquer Your Fear

Fear is conquered only in the presence of love, which is the exact opposite of fear. Here are three principles that will help you: develop trust, create a positive sense of self-worth, and change fear to positive action.

Principle #1: Develop Trust

You develop trust by doing. Every time you do something, you are building the trust that you can do it. Trust sets the foundation of doing without judging if you are doing it correctly or not. Also, when you trust that what you are doing is exactly what you are supposed to be doing, you get it done without always questioning why.

Principle #2: Create a Positive Sense of Self-Worth

When I was raising my son, my job came second. I sometimes felt people looked at me as though I was a non-achiever. I had to develop the courage to stand up for what I believed in and stay true to myself.

Self-respect means that you value yourself regardless of your job title, income, weight, age, education, or color. Encourage courage in yourself to get strong and stand up for yourself. Accept yourself just as you are and don't wish to be like anyone else.

Principle #3: Change Fear to Action

Once I decided to fulfill my destiny, things got really scary. I was afraid of what people would think, I feared failing, I feared succeeding, I felt I lacked money, I felt I lacked resources, and I thought I wasn't smart enough to become successful.

It turned around for me, though, when I made a conscious decision to accept my purpose and destiny. I realized that the experiences I went through enabled me to do this. All of my life experiences made up my purpose, and today I teach what I have learned.

You can start to change fear by inwardly becoming stronger. Dare to face the things that scare you. Don't procrastinate. Take a step toward the very thing you are afraid of. The more steps you take, the easier it gets. You are closer than you think!

Sandra's Success Secrets

Stop feeding your fear; starve it.

Be a problem-solver.

Live in the solution.

8

HOW TO

Get Motivated

*H*ow often have you made these statements about motivation: If I was motivated I could lose weight, start my own business, get out of debt, start dating, go back to school, or create a better life for myself.

Some people blame a lack of motivation for the reason they are not doing what they want to do or becoming who they want to be. If you ask them how things are going, they will tell you everything would be great if they could only get motivated!

Motivation Is Internal

The good news about motivation is that is internal. In other words, only you can motivate you. The bad news is that no one can do it for you. There is nothing outside of you that can make you do what you need to do.

Here is a true story to illustrate what I am talking about. I used to go to a high-end hair salon to get my hair cut and colored. The owner took great pride in her salon, hired top-notch stylists, and provided excellent customer service.

One Saturday I went to the salon to have my hair cut. The front desk receptionist did not greet me when I arrived because he was on the phone arguing with his girlfriend. As I stood there, he continued talking on the phone and gestured for me to sit down.

A few minutes later, my stylist came out and took me to his workstation. As I walked through the salon, I saw opened bags of chips, cans of sodas, and candy spread out all over the counters. The employees acted as if they couldn't care less about the well-respected reputation of the salon.

I asked my stylist, "Is there something special going on here today?" He smiled and replied, "Totally! We're celebrating because the owner is on vacation for a whole week!"

The owner of the salon had the employees' cooperation as long as he was present, but the minute he was absent, they did as they pleased because the boss was their motivation. The moral to the story is that every person gets to decide, based on their actions, how committed they are to a given goal.

When you decide to commit to changing your life, you take ownership and become responsible for every decision you make. Remember, you must do this on your own; no one can do it for you. You are always your own boss.

Three Secrets to Motivation

Here are three secrets to motivation: first, you must *believe* that what you do matters; second, you must *trust* that after you make a decision to do something it will happen; and third, you must *stick with it* until what you want to happen *does* happen.

If you don't believe what you want to do matters, or if you can't trust that what you want to have happen will happen, you will give up. You will go back to doing what you have always done because you know what to expect.

In the past, I was unable to commit to anything, make a decision, or believe things would work out for the best. For years I felt as if I were banging my head against a wall while wondering, "What is the matter with me?"

Things are different for me now because I learned how to motivate myself by knowing that what I am doing matters and trusting that what I want to happen will happen. In other words, I trust my destiny.

If you realize you lack trust and/or you have negative self-beliefs, find out why and work on learning how to trust yourself and actively convert all your inner thoughts to empowering, positive self-beliefs—your future depends on it. If you need help, then I hope this book will help you with that.

Uncover Your Barriers

Whether you are working, raising children, or both, your life demands can make it seem almost impossible to find a way to change your situation. I believe that is why just being told to set goals isn't the best place to start. The place to start is to figure out what barrier is keeping you from what it is you want.

Here is an example from my life. Every time I tried to start a business venture I would plan it, and then quit. Quitting made me feel stupid, hopeless, and fearful that I would end up living a life I hated. I used to say, "If I could only get motivated, I could make this happen."

The truth is that quitting didn't make me feel those things, and not being motivated didn't make me feel those things. It was my internal barriers and my inability to overcome them that made me feel those things.

To put it another way, first I needed to uncover my barriers. Then, I had to deal with my feelings of fear, hopelessness, and low self-worth by changing my negative self-beliefs to positive self-beliefs.

Please make a workbook page "Internal and External Barriers to Motivation" by photocopying the appropriate page from the appendix. You will record what it is you want, and possible barriers you might be experiencing that are affecting your chances of moving toward your dreams.

Internal and External Barriers to Motivation

Think of what you want. What is it that you want? Do you want to start a business, end a relationship, change jobs, or lose weight? Write down your answer.

My goal, desire, or dream: _____

_____

_____

_____

Think of what your barriers might be to getting what you want and list them here. I have listed some for you.

No resources	*Too stupid*
Lack of trust	*No one to help you*
Believing you can't	*Other people criticism*
Feeling of hopelessness	*Fear of success*
Anger	*Nothing ever changes*
Fear of failure	*Too tired*
Too many responsibilities	*Feeling alone*
Too old	*Guilt*
Not enough money	*Past failures*
Low self-worth	*Lack of self-respect*
Can't stay focused	

My barriers to getting what I really want:

Now that you see your goal and barriers written down, what do you think? Can you see how motivation is not the answer to accomplishing your goal? The way you accomplish your goal is to first overcome your barriers.

> *"Don't wait for motivation to get what you want, overcome the barrier that is keeping you from it."*

Overcome Your Barriers

Let's say you want to lose weight. Your plan is to eat right and exercise. Within one week you give up. You are now at a crossroads and you have two choices.

Your first choice is to give up trying to lose weight and wait for motivation to show up. The second choice is look for what barrier might be holding you back and then do whatever is necessary to take action.

I have created a diagram to help you understand this. Your first choice is shown in the motivation cycle called "I'm Stuck!" In this cycle you want to lose weight, you decide you can't because you hate to exercise, and you choose to wait for motivation. You end up back where you started, and the cycle keeps going.

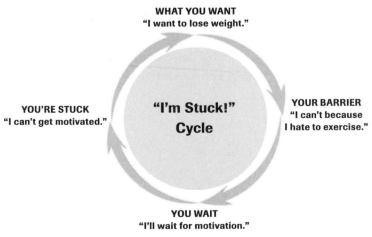

WHAT YOU WANT
"I want to lose weight."

YOU'RE STUCK
"I can't get motivated."

**"I'm Stuck!"
Cycle**

YOUR BARRIER
"I can't because
I hate to exercise."

YOU WAIT
"I'll wait for motivation."

The next motivation cycle is called "I'm Motivated!" You want to lose weight, you decide you can't because you hate to exercise, you choose to exercise, and now you are motivated because you are losing weight. Here, the negative cycle ends.

WHAT YOU WANT
"I want to lose weight."

CYCLE STOPS HERE

YOU'RE MOTIVATED
"I am motivated because
I am losing weight."

**"I'm Motivated!"
Cycle**

YOUR BARRIER
"I can't because
I hate to exercise."

ACTION TO OVERCOME BARRIER
"I choose to walk."

The cycle of no motivation ends when you choose to think about why you can't lose weight, and then choose to take action to overcome that specific barrier. I know taking action isn't always the easiest thing to do, but once you get going it will get easier.

Feel free to customize these diagrams by writing in what it is you want, your barrier, and what action you take to overcome your barrier. I have made a blank one for you to copy from the appendix for your workbook.

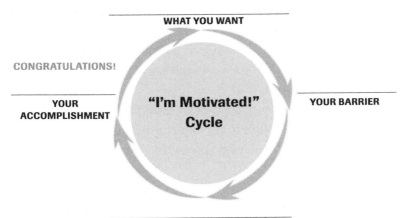

If you can adopt the concept that was explained in the diagram, I believe you will never look outside yourself for motivation again. All of your motivation will come from within you. You will choose to take action to overcome your barriers, and you will get what you really want.

Remember these three crucial ingredients to motivation:

First, you must know what you want.

Second, you must be able to identify your barrier.

Third, you must take action to overcome the barrier.

Turn Motivation into Success

Now that your internal barriers are uncovered, it's time to take action. I have provided three strategies to help you turn motivation into success.

Strategy #1: How to Decide What You Really Want

This is an often-asked question at conferences and workshops: "How can I quit doing what I don't want to do and begin doing what I want to do?" I know exactly what they are asking me because I used to ask myself the same question.

So, how do you stop doing what you don't want to do? First, you must become conscious of everything you are doing in your life that you absolutely want to quit doing. Then, you must make a decision that you will find a way to stop doing those things you don't want to do.

This isn't always easy to do, though, especially if you are a people pleaser, or if you are unable to ask for help, or if you like to always be in control, or if you spend most of your time doing for others.

What you can do about it: After you photocopy the appendix page titled "Thoughts, Beliefs, and Activities I Want to Quit/Start Doing," go to your workbook and make two lists—things you want to quit doing and things you want to start doing. Knowing what you want to quit doing is just as important as knowing what you want to begin doing.

Here is what my "quit doing" list looked like: working at a job I hate, hanging around negative people, saying "I can't," worrying that everything had to be perfect, procrastinating, and waiting for someone to come along and makes thing right.

Create your list of thoughts, beliefs, or activities you want to quit doing so you can spend more time and energy on the things you want to be doing. Procrastination will weaken its grip on you if you feel you have a choice not to do something.

Thoughts, Beliefs, and Activities
I Want to Quit/Start Doing

Thoughts, beliefs, and activities I want to quit doing:

_____

_____

_____

Thoughts, beliefs, and activities I want to start doing:

_____

_____

_____

Now, I want you to list things you want to start doing. This will provide you with a focus, something you can pour your energy and passion into so you can live an effective and successful life.

Here is what my "start doing" list looked like: I want to own a success-driven business that embraces my values, which are freedom, choice, and self-expression. I want to help other people find their purpose and destiny. And lastly, I want to believe it to the degree that it is truly possible for it to happen to me in my life.

Create your own list of things you want to start doing. This list can lead you to your path to where you want to go and what you want to do. Just reading your list after you write it can feel very empowering. That is because you are becoming more focused.

You are now focused on what is important to you, and this will motivate you to keep moving toward your dreams. It is always easier to move toward something than to constantly keep trying to move away from something.

Strategy #2: How to Stop Procrastinating

Procrastination had its ugly grip on me for much of my life. It kept me stuck in the exact place I didn't want to be. It seemed that no matter how much I tried, I couldn't shake my deep need to procrastinate. And, I could never seem to figure out why.

I procrastinated about everything: paying my bills, starting a savings program, starting a walking program, finishing up projects, doing my filing, and much more. I hated myself when I put stuff off; it made me feel lazy, stupid, and out of control.

If this sounds like you in any way, you know the frustration procrastination creates. So why do we stall? Procrastination is often a signal of inner conflict. Habitually postponing important or necessary tasks can be a way to sabotage success, avoid imagined failure, or express resentment of authority.

What you can do about it: What can you do if you are procrastinating? Get going! Getting started is the most difficult step for procrastinators, so start small. Tackle projects one part at a time. Even if you devote only fifteen minutes a day to your project, you'll see noticeable progress at the end of the week.

Here are some other ideas to help you stop procrastinating:

1. Don't wait, go attack it.

2. Don't try to be perfect, be productive.

3. Don't look for a way out, boldly go right to it.

4. Don't feel guilty if you decide not to do it.

5. Don't feel alone; get a friend to help you stay focused.

Try to get in the habit of using one of these five ideas when you feel you are procrastinating. The more determined you are to use them, the quicker it will become a habit to use them.

Strategy #3: How to Take Action

I can't tell you how many people give up on a dream because it is too hard for them to take action. It is difficult for them to accomplish their goal because first they must change an attitude, habit, or behavior.

You might need to change your attitude toward exercise, change your belief that you can't do something, or say no to someone who is taking advantage of you.

When I hear people say, "I'll exercise when I feel motivated, or "I'll apply for a better job when my self-esteem goes up," I always recommend that they not wait. I recommend they take action. Taking action is what creates motivation and raises your self-esteem.

What you can do about it: First, ask yourself, "What do I want?" You already worked this out in the exercise "Thoughts, Beliefs, and Activities I Want to Start Doing." Let's continue with the theme that you want to walk to lose weight.

Second, ask yourself, "Am I willing to do what it takes to make it happen?" If your answer is no, you don't want to walk, than accept your choice and say out loud, "I am motivated. I choose not to walk this evening." Do not sit on the sofa and call yourself lazy. If after awhile you change your mind, go and walk.

If your answer is yes, pick one thing you can begin doing immediately; in this case, go walk for fifteen minutes. While walking, feel good about the fact that you are closer to your goal of losing weight. Tell yourself "good job."

If while walking you are thinking, "I will not lose weight by walking only fifteen minutes," stop thinking that message immediately and replace it with, "I am motivated. I will lose weight. This fifteen minutes matters." Do not allow your inner critic to stop you from doing something you want to do.

On the topic of personal effectiveness someone to read is Brian Tracy. I love his book *Focal Point* because it gives you a system to achieve all your goals. He also has a great Web site that offers free weekly success newsletters.

I can honestly say that Brian Tracy's work has made quite a difference in my life. He has a way of helping people tap into their true potential. Potential is a result of work, and he shows you how to do that.

My best advice if you feel you want to wait to feel positive, motivated, or energized to do something you may not want to do is this: Don't wait for it to feel good, 'cause it won't. Just do what you have to do and get it done.

How Motivation Creates Success

The truth is that successful people aren't successful because they have high IQs, more education, or more money. *Successful people are successful because they are willing to do the very thing they don't want to do.*

Here's a great example of what I am talking about. Writing is a challenge for me because it is a solo activity and I love to be around people. My other challenge is that I find it extremely difficult to sit for long hours to read, write, and research, which I do a lot of as an author and speaker.

On mornings when writing is making me crazy, I will drive to Starbucks, grab a mocha, and chat with anyone willing to talk to me. I usually stay about an hour, and then head back to my home office.

This one morning I was completely stressed-out because the writing wasn't going so well. Even though my hair was dirty, I had no makeup on, and I was wearing ten-year-old sweatpants, I decided I needed go to Starbucks and talk to Dave, my favorite Starbucks employee. We always talk about my book while he makes my mocha.

I walked in and ordered my drink. He took one look at me and said, "Sandra, you look exhausted." I rolled my eyes and said, "I *am* exhausted." He asked, "How long have you been in your office working on your book this morning?" I answered miserably, "For thirty-five minutes!"

Dave started laughing. He didn't see how writing for just thirty-five minutes could be so exhausting. Well, that is a long time for someone who hates to write! You see, when you do what you love, all day can feel like minutes. And when you do what you don't like to do, minutes can feel like all day.

The way I see it, lack of motivation is when you know you need to do something, but you can't seem to get yourself to do it. Motivation is when you can make yourself do the very thing you don't want to do.

This book is proof positive that I motivated myself to sit for long hours and write. I turned down many speaking engagements, worked in my office twelve hours a day, and kept my focus on one singular activity—writing.

I was motivated to write this book because I believed that it mattered, and I trusted that this book would happen because it was my destiny. Your belief in destiny protects your destiny, no matter what you go through.

Embrace Self-Love

I believe the biggest barrier to motivation is a lack of self-love. When you place harsh judgment on your own thoughts and actions, you minimize the importance of who you are, your life, and what you aspire to do with it.

When you tell yourself what you do doesn't matter, isn't important enough, or won't change anything anyway, it can knock motivation right out of you. This type of thinking defeats your spirit.

The truth is that everything you do matters. It matters what you think, feel, act, say, and do. You must believe you are doing what you are meant to do, and you must believe that you have the ability to do it.

Your future is not ahead of you; it's trapped inside of you. Decide what steps you need to take, get motivated, and get going. Love yourself enough to get what you really want and live the life you were meant to live.

Sandra's Success Secrets

Motivation is internal.

It only takes one small step to take action.

Believe in yourself;
then be around people who believe in you.

9

Eliminate Clutter

When I finally got off of welfare, I worked full time and sometimes even worked a second job part-time to make ends meet. After being gone all day, I would come home tired and try to straighten up my apartment. I would look around and think, "I hate this place!"

It was decorated and furnished with ugly second-hand furniture. Nothing seemed to go together and the space didn't feel warm and inviting. Every time I walked through the front door, I dreaded the thought of having to spend time there.

To add insult to injury, I compared my mother's beautiful and clean house to my dumpy apartment. She worked hard to always keep everything spotless. When she had company over they would say, "Dorie, your house is so clean you can eat off the floor!"

You can clearly see that my problems were much greater than just needing to get rid of physical clutter. I also had mental and emotional clutter, such as stress, feeling broke, and having too much to do as a single mom.

Pay close attention to what is going on in your life as you work on getting rid of clutter. Often, so much of what is happening inside of you shows up outside of you. For instance, if you fear moving on, you will somehow misplace or lose an application for a new, promising job and you miss the opportunity to apply.

What Your Home Says about You

Look around your home and ask yourself, "How do I feel when I'm in this space?" When you are in your bedroom, do you feel safe and nurtured? When you are in your bathroom, is it a place where you can experience privacy and renewal?

When you are in your dining room, can you relax and enjoy your meal? What is the focus in your main living area? Is the television the main focus?

If someone were to enter your home, how would they describe you based on your interior design? In other words, what does your home say about you? This exercise is really fun to do. Just photocopy the appendix page and insert it into your workbook when you are finished.

What My Home Says about Me

_____

_____

_____

Now, would you say that your home expresses who you really are?

_____

If yes, why? _____

If no, why? _____

Here are more questions about the individual rooms in your house:

My bedroom feels _____

My kitchen feels _____

My living room feels _____

My bathroom feels _____

Look at all your answers. Do they express a feeling of warmth or icy cold? Calm or chaos? Clean or cluttered? Become aware of the feelings your personal space evokes in you because you are going to want to change what you don't like.

Clutter

Everyone has it and everyone hates it. You probably have stacks of magazines you haven't had time to read, clothes you haven't worn in a long time but you hope to wear again, and boxes of books from your college days.

Perhaps you inherited someone's stuff and you don't have the heart to get rid of it. Maybe you love to shop too much and your closet is full of things that still have the tags on them.

Maybe you are the person who can't say no, so people turn to you when they need to store their stuff. Or maybe you buy duplicates of everything because you worry about not having enough.

You might have things you are emotionally connected to and have a hard time parting with. Maybe you got a birthday gift you know you will never wear, but wouldn't feel right discarding. If any of these apply to you, help is on the way.

How Clutter Affects Your Life

Let's say you need to balance your bank statement. When your workspace at home is organized, you can easily find your paperwork and get your bank statement balanced within minutes.

When your home office is disorganized, it takes just as much time to find the paperwork as it takes for you to do the paperwork. Now it takes you twice as much time and energy to balance your bank statement.

Let's say you have an important report due by tomorrow. When your workspace at your office is organized, you find the report, place it on your desk the night before, and start on it first thing in the morning.

Again, let's say an important report is due by tomorrow. You leave your office a mess and show up in the morning. You waste time trying to find the report, you give up looking, and decide to head to the break room for coffee. Now it takes you twice as much time and energy to complete your report.

When things are left undone, when you can see stuff you need to get rid of, and when you constantly think about everything you need to do but aren't doing, it drains your energy and steals your precious time.

On the other hand, when you are organized and you get stuff done quickly, you now have extra time for yourself: to exercise, read, or go on a date with your sweetheart. And taking time to enjoy these types of activities helps you feel energized and good about yourself.

It's time to start getting rid of stuff. Anything that no longer serves you is what I consider clutter. You will have to decide for yourself what you want to keep and what you want to get rid of. Use your gut as your guide.

Three-Step Quick-Start System to Clear Clutter

With this system in place, you can have your home cleared of clutter in no time at all. Here are the three steps with detailed instructions on implementing each step.

1. Look at each room and mentally divide it into mini areas.

2. Decide which room you want to de-clutter first.

3. Tackle the mini areas until each room is cleared of clutter.

Step 1: Divide Each Room into Mini Areas

Stand in one room of your home, look at the room as a whole, then mentally divide and group the room into mini areas. For example, in your bedroom the first mini area could be a five-drawer dresser. Your nightstands and under the bed could be a second mini area. Your closet could be a third mini area.

Go through each room of your home this way. The exception would be a room that is occupied by someone responsible for his or her own space. For instance, there is no need to go into a room where someone is renting from you.

Step 2: Choose a Room

I suggest you start in a room with the least amount of clutter so you can see the results quicker, which will keep you motivated to do more. I started in my bathroom. Believe me, nothing feels better than getting that first room done!

Step 3: Clean the Mini Areas

Using the example in step 1, you have picked your bedroom. Now pick one mini area within that room. Let's say you pick bedroom mini area #1, which is the five-drawer dresser. Clean out one drawer of the five-drawer dresser for fifteen minutes once a week until your dresser is done.

Then do bedroom mini area #2, which are the nightstands and under the bed. Clean for fifteen minutes once a week until the area under your bed and the nightstands are done.

Finish your last bedroom mini area, #3, which is the closet. Work on your closet for fifteen minutes once a week until it's done. Guess what? Your bedroom is done!

Here is a recap of the simple process:

- Pick one room.

- Pick one mini area in that room.

- Clean out clutter for fifteen minutes once a week.

How to Clean Mini Areas

The best way to clean mini areas is to group everything into three piles: must keep, get rid of, and hold for six months.

Must keep: These are all the things you simply cannot get rid of. They are important and irreplaceable. Be careful here, though, that you're not holding on to things like photos of old boyfriends because they can have a negative effect on your current relationship. Items like these can carry an emotional memory and they might service you better in the "get rid of" pile.

Get rid of: These things have got to go. You no longer need them. Recycle or donate them to your favorite charity. There are lots of people in need and your stuff can help them.

This pile includes things you think you "should" keep. These are gifts from relatives that you don't want and will never use. Give them away. Don't feel guilty for doing so, either. It's just the way it is—gifts symbolize love, not burden.

How often do you end up with duplicates of something? This can happen when we replace something but don't get rid of the item we no longer use. If you find your space is filled with unnecessary duplicates, get rid of the duplicates.

Hold for six months: When you're going through your things and you run across something that you don't think you must keep but you're not ready to get rid of it, put it in your "hold for six months" pile.

Just like it says, hold the stuff for six months and if you end up not using or not needing those items, get rid of them. I know I have a pile of things that emotionally I am not ready to get rid of yet.

De-cluttering Tips

- This system works because you clear out clutter in small increments; which makes the job manageable. What doesn't work is seeing a room as one big pile of clutter and then thinking you have to clean out the whole room at one time. No one has the time or energy for that.

- De-clutter for about fifteen minutes at a time. After fifteen minutes, stop and put the undone stuff back where it belongs, then return to your regular activities. You always have the option of increasing or changing the amount of time you de-clutter.

- Look for every small window of time in your week that you can clear cutter. It might be some weird time like Thursday evening from 8:50 p.m to 9:05 p.m. If possible, try to create a ritual of clearing clutter at about the same time and same day each week.

- There will come a time when you will be tempted to only clear clutter when you have one big block of time. I recommend you do not do that because (1) that big block of time rarely becomes available, and (2) if it does, you run the risk of feeling overwhelmed by the size of the project and give up.

- The exception to clearing more than your fifteen minutes is when you have a little extra time and you're just about through with a mini area. For instance, the last two drawers in a dresser. Things can get exciting when you know you are just about finished!

- If it is time to do your fifteen minutes and you don't want to do it because you feel crabby, stick to your plan and do it anyway. Remember, it's only fifteen minutes. Believe me, the benefits of getting it done far outweigh your not doing it.

- Motivate yourself! Play a Tina Turner CD while you work.

- When you sort stuff, put pressure on yourself to go through it quickly. Pick up something, put it in a pile, and move on.

- The more you work with this system, it easier it gets.

- If your stomach feels funny while you are clearing clutter, this is a normal reaction to releasing an object that you are emotionally connected to. Acknowledge your icky feelings, and then continue working.

- The number one reason why people accumulate so much stuff is because they lack the time and energy to deal with it.

- Don't wait for the "right" time or "right" day to clear out clutter. With your busy life, that right day or time never happens. Just find little mini pockets of time and the dedication to get it done.

- The truth is: When your life is organized and clutter-free, you can get what you really want—without the guilt.

Clear Clutter Worksheet

I made a worksheet to help you clear clutter using the three-step quick-start system. I also made an example for you to follow. Once you get rolling on this, it will be so exciting to check the box "completed"! And once you are done with all the rooms, your house won't feel or look the same. You can find the "Clear Clutter Worksheet" in the appendix, photocopy it for as many rooms as you have in your house, and insert the sheets to work on in your workbook. I know it will be a challenge to find the extra time and energy to clear out clutter and organize your home and/or office. If you hang with it, though, it will get done. And remember, the sooner you get started, the sooner you will finish.

Clear Clutter Worksheet

Example:
ROOM: Bedroom

MINI AREA #1	MINI AREA #2	MINI AREA #3
Dresser	*Nightstands, under the bed*	*Closet*
Completed!	*Completed!*	*Completed!*

Mind Clutter

What is mind clutter? It is mental clutter, images you can't seem to get out of your brain, negative thinking, and old tapes of past negative experiences that you constantly replay in your mind—that is mind clutter!

Mind clutter can keep you stuck because you keep replaying the past. If you do try to do something daring and new, your mind clutter will feed you the negative message "Don't try, you will fail."

If this goes unchecked, the possibility of you getting what you really want will be jeopardized. That's because mind clutter is so powerful, and it operates most of time in your subconscious.

Realize that when you think a negative thought over and over with the belief that it is true, it becomes true whether it is true or not. And those negative thoughts affect your behavior.

For instance, you show up at work and pass by your boss. She is busy working on an important task and does not look up to say good morning to you. Your mind takes over and starts thinking thoughts such as "She doesn't like me," "I bet she is going to get me fired," and then, "Oh my gosh, I am going to lose my job!"

Your thoughts turned into a mental image so powerful that you went from not getting a simple hello to losing your job. And, if you continue thinking those thoughts, soon they take up residency in your brain.

Ways to Deal with Mind Clutter

For you to get what you really want, you must deal with your negative mind clutter. Here are ways to do that:

- For one week, be the observer and become conscious of all the thoughts rolling around in your head.

- Write down on paper those thoughts you feel are negative and are getting in your way of you moving forward. You can do this in your workbook.

- When you think a negative thought, immediately say, "Stop!" and replace it with an empowering thought.

- Reread chapter one, "How to Transform Beliefs."

Principles Related to Mind Clutter

Four mind clutter principles:

1. Learn to let go.

2. Let life wake you up.

3. Identify the thought before the action.

4. Potent thoughts become visible.

Emotional Clutter

Lastly, there is emotional clutter. This is in your heart zone where all of your feelings and emotions reside. If your heart is filled with self-love and love for others, you will attract and deal with loving energy in your life.

If you are filled with negative emotional clutter, you will experience emotions such as fear, hate, anger, jealousy, an unwillingness to forgive, or revenge, and you will continue to attract and deal with negative energy in your life.

Ways to Deal with Emotional Clutter

- Change your energy to self-love by practicing self-care.

- Have unconditional self-respect for yourself regardless if you can or cannot do something.

- Replace old tapes with new images of your current successes.

- Forgive yourself for what you think you should have done and forgive others for what they have done.

- Stop jealousy in its tracks by seeing yourself as successful and wanting the same for others.

- Success is not success without love.

- Rethink and rewrite all messages that no longer serve you.

- My personal favorite: tell someone you love him or her.

Principles Related to Emotional Clutter

Seven emotional clutter principles:

1. Love and fear are opposing forces.

2. What we need to learn, we attract.

3. Know your own forgiveness.

4. Anger comes from fear.

5. Fear is an emotion that makes what is false seem real.

6. Trying to get revenge only hurts you.

7. What is happening around you isn't as important as what is inside you.

Creating Sacred Space

Do you love to crawl into bed at night because your sheets are soft and cozy? When you grab a pan in the morning to scramble some eggs, is the pan easy to find? Do you love the color of your bathroom?

If you answered no, you are not alone. People everywhere are desperate for ways to organize their lives and create places they love. That is why there are so many great books on the topic of clutter, simplicity living, time management, and feng shui.

Ultimately, you want your living space to embrace and reflect who you are. It isn't about used furniture, expensive furniture, or if the space is spotless. It is about you walking in your front door and immediately feeling embraced and connected to the space.

That is what is known as sacred space. Sacred space is an environment that envelops you with nourishment and support and helps you bring something new and wonderful into your life.

This idea of creating sacred space has caught on for a lot of people. They have created specific areas within their homes to renew, refresh, and replenish: big sunken tubs, reading rooms, lots of beautiful lighting, and rich colors on the walls.

Within that nourishing and calm environment, they entertain, take a college course online, operate a home-based business, home-school their children, exercise in a home gym, and watch videos on their flat-screen TVs.

How do you create sacred space? It is created through intention. This means that you intentionally clean, decorate, and live in your house with the intent of manifesting something that you want. Clearing out clutter and using the principles of feng shui can help you do that.

If you want to read more about intention, I recommend *The Power of Intention* by Dr. Wayne W. Dyer. The author of this book teaches you how to tap into transformational energy. He also presents *The Power of Intention* on PBS television. If it's on in your area, try to watch it.

Sacred space can be internal and/or external. For example, you can go inward to your sacred space and use your thoughts to conjure up wonderful images to calm you when you get stressed.

I have trained myself to do this and I am quite good at it. For instance, when I am on a trip I can go to my inner space while waiting for my flight, while on my flight, or on the shuttle bus that takes me to my hotel.

Sacred space is also a physical place in your home. You go there to be alone to meditate, pray, journal, dance, chant, or listen to music. Some people place candles or incense along with fragrant flowers in their sacred space. You can put a favorite picture there, keep your journal there, or simply leave it bare.

If space is an issue, no problem. You can set up your sacred space in a corner of a room. It can be at the end of your bed. It doesn't matter where it is; just make sure you feel safe and nurtured there.

In the beginning, I recommend you spend a minimum of ten minutes once a day in your sacred space. Do that for the first month, and then increase your time to whatever you are comfortable with. The benefits of taking time just for you are astounding; you become balanced, centered, and creative.

While in your sacred space think about what it is you want with the intention that you will manifest it. You can do this a number of ways. You can chant one word over and over, you can repeat affirmations, or clear your mind to complete stillness.

A great book on this topic is *Creating Sacred Space with Feng Shui* by Karen Kingston. It helped me understand and embrace the power of intention. She also talks about feng shui, clutter, and space clearing.

Feng Shui

Feng shui teaches the power of intention and the placement of things to fulfill your wishes. When you set a goal with the intent of achieving it, and place specific items in your home as a reinforcement of your wishes, you are practicing or using feng shui.

I have come up with four powerful intentions and examples of how you can use feng shui in your own home.

Four Powerful Intentions for Your Home

1. Express who you are becoming. If you are a server in a restaurant who aspires to be an artist, hang your art on a wall in your home. If you work in customer service around lots of people and you want to become a researcher in a library, create a personal space that is quiet and filled with books. Let your space express who you are becoming.

2. Express what you want to attract. If you are alone and you are looking for a relationship, place a vase of fresh red flowers in your bedroom. Put gold coins in an attractive container to attract wealth. Post a picture of the BMW you want on your refrigerator. Let your space express what you want to attract.

3. Express your authentic self. If you see your true self as deeply spiritual, paint a wall purple. If you are meticulous, organize your space to be functional. If you are whimsical and your rule is to live life without rules, swing the windows open, crank up your favorite CD, and dance the night away. Let your space express your authentic self.

4. Express your intention to prosper and grow. If your intention is to have caring people in your life, get rid of pictures of your toxic ex-boyfriend. If your intention is to raise your sense of self, get rid of an old book and buy a new book on self-improvement. If your intention is to climb the corporate ladder, gift your old clothes to men and women getting off of welfare. Let your space express your intention to prosper and grow.

If the topic of Feng Shui is of interest to you, there are a lot of great books on the subject. One of my favorites is *Move Your Stuff, Change Your Life* by Karen Rauch Carter. She has a way of explaining feng shui that makes it easy to understand.

Chapter Recap

This chapter began by asking you to pay close attention to what is going on in your life as you clear clutter. Sometimes clutter represents something more than just being messy.

Clutter sometimes serves as a mirror of a bigger problem. I am not suggesting you not clear up the clutter. I am suggesting you look a little deeper at what you might be experiencing and deal with those issues as well.

Next, you were asked to take a step back and look at your home as if you were a stranger. There was an exercise that asked you to describe the type of person who lives in your home.

Clutter was the next topic. You learned there are three types of clutter: physical clutter, mind clutter, and emotional clutter. You learned how to clear clutter by creating mini areas, received lots of de-cluttering tips and ways to deal with clutter, and learned clutter principles.

Then sacred space and intention were explained. You learned what they were and how you can create sacred space for yourself.

Lastly, you learned how feng shui and intention are connected, the four powerful intentions, and examples of how to activate intention in your own home.

Sandra's Success Secrets

Everything you own, owns you.

Your outer world reflects your inner world.

***Get rid of what you don't want
to make room for what you do want.***

94

10

═══ **HOW TO** ═══

Find Time

If you are challenged with time management issues, and you want to dig a little deeper to find out why, this chapter will give you an opportunity to do just that. You will be surprised to see what can hold you back.

We won't be focusing on time management because you probably already have information on that. We will be focusing on you and how you can effectively manage your life to go for your dreams.

We will begin by looking at how your personality is reflected in the way you handle time. In other words, you have personal characteristics that either help or hinder your ability to manage time well.

What Holds You Back

Here are seven personal characteristics that can *hinder* your ability to use time well. See if you relate to any of them.

1. Perfectionism
2. Fear of success
3. Lack of confidence
4. Need to be loved
5. Poor self-image
6. Self-sabotage
7. Need for control

Perfectionism

Perfectionism is tricky to deal with because many business environments believe this to be an excellent employee trait. The fact is that perfectionism can hold up timelines and create stress in the person who struggles with perfectionism.

Perfectionism can sometimes be tied to a childhood in which the child received large doses of disapproval, ridicule, or rejection. When the young person is constantly criticized, he or she becomes hypersensitive and is driven to be perfect to avoid the criticism. As an adult, the person is driven to produce perfect work, relationships, or self.

When we look at personality profiling, we see that perfectionists fit into one of the four quadrants. They are called the Thinkers. They are hardwired to be structured, methodical, and factual. In other words, they need more time to do their thing.

When a Thinker is out of balance, thinking consumes them. They are no longer utilizing their intuition, creativity, or interpersonal skills. They are compulsively processing over and over data and information. This imbalance of using thinking skills can only create tremendous stress for this person.

Another outcome of perfectionism is compulsive review. Just like it sounds, a person compulsively reviews information over and over in his or her head, even long after the workday is over.

A remedy for perfectionism is to do a project and find a finish point and stop. Tell yourself that you can always go back later and change something, but for right now it's good enough. Of course, this will feel horrible when you do it.

Overcoming perfectionism frees you to get more done in your day, helps you enlist your intuition, and provides opportunities to engage in more interpersonal relationships in your personal and professional life.

The bottom line for time management: Perfectionism causes difficulty in allotting time for projects.

Fear of Success

Fear of success was discussed in chapter seven and needs to be in this chapter as well because it is considered a personal characteristic that hinders your use of time. And the best time management system in the world can't help you if you fear success.

Fear of success is when you feel you do not deserve success so you help yourself fail. Not only do you need to believe you deserve success, but you must also believe that you deserve what it is you are going after, or you will not have it.

You see, believe deep in your core that you deserve to be successful and you will become successful. If you don't, you will find it difficult to stay on track, complete things, or motivate yourself when you need it.

Overcome your fear. Don't let it stop you. Study chapter one to help you with your beliefs and chapter seven on fear. Get some other books and study those as well. You can handle your fear and move toward your dreams.

The bottom line for time management: Fear of success leads to wasting time through procrastination.

Lack of Confidence

If you find it almost impossible for you to make up your mind, it could be because you lack confidence. When you feel you aren't qualified enough or smart enough, you can end up questioning your every decision.

When you are at work and someone asks for your opinion, if you have one, let her hear what you have to say. When it is time to make a decision, make one and move on. Don't spend your whole evening worrying if you made the right decision or not.

Strengthen your confidence with self-respect. Self-respect means you accept yourself unconditionally, whether you can or cannot do something.

Don't wait to develop confidence on the inside before you show confidence on the outside. Stand your ground and look confident, whether you are or not. No one knows your heart is pounding and your knees are shaking. Always remember, people only believe what they see.

Chapter five can help you look confident through empowered communication skills.

Bottom line to time management: Lack of confidence causes indecisiveness, a major time-waster.

Need to Be Loved

If you need to be loved and you look for it at work, chances are you are willing to do whatever anyone wants you to do with the hope that it will fill your need for love. You will volunteer for projects you don't have time for, stay late when you need to be home, and be the only person to make coffee at work even though thirty-five people work there.

Don't look outside yourself for love because you are looking in the wrong place. The truth is, self-love is where you find love. And when you are filled with love for yourself and your life, you will attract like energy.

Chapter five on communications can help you learn how to speak up, and chapter six can help you handle your emotions.

Bottom line to time management: The need to be loved leads to an inability to say "no" to time-wasters such as unscheduled visitors, phone calls, and unnecessary requests for help.

Poor Self-Image

Feeling inadequate can undermine your self-image. Self-image is an internal image of how you see yourself—and how you see yourself affects how others see you. Sometimes, when you don't feel good about yourself and treat yourself poorly, others will treat you poorly as well.

There is a direct correlation between low self-worth and/or

self-value and negative self-talk. If most of your internal messages are negative, you must convert them to positive messages to raise your sense of self. You are what you think you are.

Go back to chapter one for help on how to convert negative internal messages into positive empowering messages.

Bottom line to time management: Poor self-image fosters difficulty setting priorities and using time efficiently, due to fear of being thought inadequate.

Self-Sabotage

When you don't believe you truly deserve what you want in life, you can sabotage your chances for obtaining your goals. People who believe they are bad may make themselves fail in order to ensure the punishment they think they deserve.

Never completing a project, getting the project in late, or hurrying to do a project at the last minute might be a sign of self-sabotage. Don't allow that to happen. Uncover why you are stalling and create a strategy to get stuff done.

Stop sabotaging your chances of living the life you were meant to live. Don't set yourself up for failure. Expect that you will succeed.

The bottom line for time management: Poor time management becomes a tool for self-sabotage.

Need for Control

When you do for others and you have an inability to delegate work, that's need for control. When you seem to think you are the only one who can do your job at work and at home, and that no one else is capable of doing it, that's a need for control.

Keeping busy, being in control, and doing everything yourself can make you feel valued. It also takes the attention off the fact that you are not working on things that can move you toward your own dreams.

Look at what you're doing from a different perspective. Think about what it is you want out of life and start eliciting other people's help. Heck, if you weren't so busy volunteering for all those extra projects, what other cool things could you be doing?

The bottom line for time management: Need for control often causes refusal to delegate work.

——

That completes the seven personal characteristics that hinder your use of time. Identify which ones you need to work on. See them as habits that can be changed. Understand that when you remove obstacles, you make way for a life that is rich and rewarding.

What Gets You Going

Now that we've talked about seven personal characteristics that hinder your ability to manage time well, let's talk about seven personal characteristics that *help* you use your time well.

Together, these make up your personal life management system. It is a *personal* system because it only fits you, a *life* system because it encompasses your personal and professional life, and a *management* system because it helps guide you to what you want.

Because these ideas are discussed in other chapters, I have summarized the information. Here are the seven characteristics that help your ability to use time well:

1. Thoughts
2. Beliefs
3. Values
4. Goals
5. Choices
6. Actions
7. Energy

Thoughts and Beliefs

Your thoughts and beliefs are the beginning of all creative ideas and all roadblocks. If you believe you can do something, you can. If you believe you can't, you can't. That is where it all begins, with your thoughts.

Values and Goals

Your values guide your goals, and when you pursue a goal you are making decisions based on your values. You get to decide what type of person you want to be and what you believe in. Any activity that goes counter to your values will not be part of your plan.

Choices and Actions

You exercise your choices when you decide what you want to do and what you do not want to do. For instance, do you take action and speak up, or do you stay silent? Do you take action and go back to school, or stay in your current job? Your choices help you decide what action to take.

Energy

The last component to your personal life management system is energy. It takes energy to walk every day. It takes energy to study. It takes energy to clear out clutter. And without energy to help you move forward on your dreams, you will get stuck.

Now that we have discussed the seven characteristics, I want to spend a little more time discussing the topic of energy. Wouldn't you agree that nothing is more discouraging than wanting to do something but not finding the energy to do it?

Through my years of frustration over my lack of time management skills, I discovered a correlation between how much personal energy I had and how I used my time. This discovery was a big turning point for me.

Personal Energy

Here what's tricky about personal energy:

- It's in short supply when you live a busy life.
- It is almost impossible to go after what it is you want without it.

Your reaction to what I just said might be: "Sandra is right! How can I go for my dreams when I can barely get through the day?" I hear this more times than not from women and men who attend my seminars.

I totally understand that reaction because my life used to leave me feeling the same way. Raising a son on my own and being the breadwinner left me few options. It seemed like all I did was go to work, come home, and work some more.

The way you find time is to find more energy. Tap into your personal energy and you can do just about anything you want or need to do. "How do you do that?" you ask. Well, you do that by decreasing your energy drainers and increasing your energy boosters.

Energy Drainers

An energy drainer is any thought, belief, or action that leaves you feeling hopeless, unmotivated, or stressed. They can be negative thoughts stuck deep in your subconscious mind, negative beliefs you say to yourself, or everyday activities that drive you crazy.

I have created an exercise to help you identify all the things in your life that drain your energy. Earlier you created a section in your workbook for this chapter, "How to Find Time." Now copy the page from the appendix named "Energy Drainers." Check the energy drainers that apply to you and your life.

Energy Drainers

These take away your energy:

_____ Lack of time	_____ Working at a job I hate
_____ Negativity	_____ Conflict and confrontation
_____ Self-doubt	_____ Toxic relationships
_____ Lack of direction	_____ Caring for aging parents
_____ An inability to say "no"	_____ Lack of faith
_____ Guilt	_____ Weight issues
_____ Victim mentality	_____ Always tired
_____ Feel I have no choices	_____ Can't sleep well at night
_____ Too many low-level activities like housework and chores	_____ Too old
_____ Stress	_____ Inconsiderate people
_____ Feeling I'm never good enough	_____ Procrastination
_____ Judgmental self-labeling like stupid, selfish, or lazy	_____ Lack of belief
_____ Living up to others' standards	_____ Old bad habits
_____ Lack of self-respect, self-value, or self-worth	_____ Worry
_____ Poor health	_____ Lack of education
_____ Always doing for others and never for myself	_____ Can't stop thinking about things and take action
_____ Lack of money	_____ Lack of self-acceptance
_____ Too concerned about what others think of me	_____ Change
_____ Loneliness	_____ Anger
_____ Fear of failure or fear of success	_____ Insecurity
	_____ Unhealthy habits
	_____ Lack of trust

How did it feel when you did this exercise? Did it drain your energy? If it did, you experienced firsthand how your energy drainers are draining energy from your life; the very energy you need to go for your dreams.

So, what is the answer? How can you deal with your energy drainers? The answer is to protect your energy that sits within your personal life management system. If you can learn to do this, you will find time.

Energy Boosters

The way you protect your energy is to participate in energy boosters. An energy booster is any thought, belief, or action that makes you feel motivated and energized. Heck, just reading the list of energy boosters in this next exercise is energizing!

I have created a list of these for you to look over. Please copy this page from the appendix for your workbook. Check off the energy boosters you already have, and put a star next to the ones you want to have.

Energy Boosters

These add to your energy:

_____ When I get stuff done

_____ Hopefulness

_____ Recognition

_____ Rewards

_____ Seeing others happy

_____ Feeling good about myself

_____ Having time off from work

_____ Balance

_____ Contentment

_____ Joy

_____ Success: Financial, occupational, relational, personal

_____ Having fun

_____ Health

_____ Losing weight

_____ Being with family and/or friends

_____ Good food

_____ Security

_____ Intimacy with my partner

_____ Being creative

_____ Alone time

_____ Overcoming an obstacle

_____ Love

_____ Meditating or praying

_____ Journaling

_____ Looking in the mirror and liking what I see

_____ Participating in hobbies I enjoy

_____ Living in a space that feels clean and organized

_____ Happiness

_____ Feeling a divine connection to a higher power

_____ Loving myself unconditionally

_____ Learning new things

_____ Climbing the corporate ladder

_____ Control

_____ Children

_____ Self-fulfillment

_____ A retirement plan

_____ Encouraging other people

_____ Making good choices

_____ Working at a job I love

_____ Having a dream

_____ Being in nature

_____ Travel

_____ Better family relationships

_____ Doing something good that helps others

_____ Fulfilling my destiny

_____ Money

_____ Goals

_____ Pets

_____ Knowing my purpose in life

_____ Shopping

_____ Humor and laughter

_____ Passion

_____ Getting remarried

_____ Optimism

_____ Music

How do you feel now? A little more energized? I hope so. This exercise helped you identify how many energy boosters you have and which ones you want to have. The bottom line is that you cannot get rid of all your energy drainers, but you can balance them with energy boosters.

How to Find Time

Since the title of this chapter is "How to Find Time," I'd better address that now. Here are three steps to finding more time. We will also be doing a little review of what you have already learned.

The first way to begin finding time is to decrease the amount of energy drainers on your list. For instance, if being around toxic people is checked off, end the relationship(s). Or, if you have an inability to say "no," start speaking up.

Second, increase the energy boosters found on your list. For instance, if being in nature is an energy booster but you are not taking walks, add a ten-minute walk to your daily routine. Every time you begin doing something on your energy booster list, you create energy.

Third, recognize and accept what you can and can't control. For instance, if on your energy drainers' list you checked off illness, obviously you cannot control the fact that you have an illness.

What you can do, though, is go to your energy booster list and do a number of things that can improve your situation. You can meditate, pray, or connect with someone you love; all of these can help you in a healthful and positive way.

If procrastination is one of your energy drainers, use the tools provided in this book to stop procrastinating. If you are caring for aging parents and it is a strain on all of your resources, find acceptance for your difficult situation. Remember, love is an energy booster.

As time goes on, be aware of when you are dealing with energy drainers or energy boosters. Be diligent about decreasing energy drainers and increasing energy boosters in small increments every day.

Remember, time management manages your time and personal management manages your energy. It takes energy to get stuff done. If you can find a way to focus and take charge of your energy, then ultimately you will find more time.

Nightstand Messages

If you are looking for something to give you strength, get you energized, and keep you focused on what you want, place a powerful message on your nightstand. Read it the moment you get up and the last thing before you fall asleep.

I realize this idea sounds kind of simple, but this one tip has done more good for keeping me pumped up than any other tip I have. That's because a "nightstand message" is what you envision for yourself.

Look over the following messages and pick the one that speaks to you. Write that message on a small piece of paper and tape it on your nightstand. If you don't see one you like, write your own. My nightstand message reads "Trust my destiny."

- I accept all of my choices; the ones that got me where I am and ones I have yet to choose.

- I will create a new mindset about working at a job I hate. It is, "I love myself and my life."

- I am my own CEO. I am my own boss.

- I have decided to be happy.

- I am focused on how I manage me.

- I will go for what I want regardless of whether I am at the perfect job, in the perfect relationship, or at the perfect weight.

- I am in a state of gratitude and I love everything I have in my life.

- I am creating new habits and throwing out old habits that aren't serving me any longer.

- I will make an exciting plan for tomorrow regardless of how my life looks today.

- I will work in my workbook, track my progress, and celebrate every inch of my personal and professional growth.

- I am doing more activities that bring me personal satisfaction.

- I say "no" when I need to say no.

- I do what I do without the guilt.

- I will grow and change and drop the problems I had last year.

- I will help myself by reading books, listening to tapes, and attending seminars.

- I will go to someone I trust, tell this person my goals, and ask for his or her love and support.

- I will live my life fully and with joy.

How Personal Management Creates Success

There are two undeniable truths about success. The first is that success is the sum of small efforts, and secondly, it's hard to succeed when all your time and effort is spent doing low-level activities. In order to succeed, you must master your time and energy.

Truth #1: Success Is the Sum of Small Efforts

I want to tell you about a woman I met when I was speaking in San Diego, California. She walked up to me at break and said, "Hi, I'm forty-four years old, I have a newborn baby, and I love to crochet."

I said, "How wonderful. I am so happy for you. Are you happy?" She replied, "No, not really." So I asked, "Why?" She said again, "Because I'm forty-four years old, I have a newborn baby, and I love to crochet."

"Well, what is the problem?" I asked.

"I stopped crocheting," she said.

"Why have you stopped crocheting?" I asked.

Looking frustrated she said, "Because I have a newborn baby!"

I told her to go home and measure out one arm's length of yarn and crochet that amount after the baby goes to bed. Now, let me ask you, do you think that is enough crocheting for one evening for a woman who is crazy for crocheting?

The answer is yes! It may not seem like a lot, but it is better than nothing. You make a huge mistake thinking that you must wait for lots of time to do something you love because more often than not, that time never comes.

When you always forgo what you love in order to take care of others, it can leave you drained, angry, and a victim of your circumstances. Pursue the things you love: dancing, drawing, walking, meditating, time with loved ones, reading a good book, or gardening.

How do you include these activities in your already busy schedule? First, think about what one small step or one activity you want to do. Could you buy a book? Take a class? Take a walk after dinner?

Secondly, look at your daily schedule for a ten- to twenty-minute slot where you can slip in that one small activity. Read for fifteen minutes or garden for twenty minutes. You can always do the activity longer as your time and schedule allow.

Ultimately, it is your responsibility to keep that special part of you alive because it shows others that you respect yourself, it increases your energy, and it makes you a happier person. Doing what you love is the way to love your life.

Truth #2: Low-Level Activities Keep You from What Is Important

Here is a typical day in the life of a working person: Go to work all day, come home, throw Costco lasagna in the oven, and clean out the kitty litter box. Next day go to work all day, come home, boil water for macaroni and cheese, and clean out the kitty litter box.

In other words, your day is filled with too many activities that are repetitive, draining, and stressful. This situation leaves you feeling stuck because you don't have enough time or energy to go after what you really want in life.

Having too much to do and not enough time to do it can squash the life right out of you. It makes you feel like whatever you do isn't enough, and if you do find an extra minute to do something nice for yourself, you feel guilty about it.

These repetitive activities are called low-level activities. They are things you must do, but they don't bring you much satisfaction, joy, or happiness. They keep you running the moment you get up in the morning and continue until it's time to go to bed.

Think about everything you do in a day. How many low-level activities are you responsible for? Do you cook, clean, run kids around, shop, balance the bank statement, get your oil changed, and clean out the garage? Record them on the "My Daily Activities" page, which you can copy from the appendix.

My Daily Activities

_____

_____

_____

_____

_____

_____

Now that you have listed your low-level activities, let's talk about what you can do about the items on the list. Here are some ideas:

- Ask for help.

- Delegate jobs to others.

- Say no when you need to.

- Do the activities quicker.

- Don't wait, just do it.

- Don't try to be perfect.

- Decide that enough is enough.

- Stop doing activities you don't need to do.

These tips sound easy to do but they are not. That's because many times life leaves you with few choices and/or resources. For instance, you might not be able to get anyone to help you, or maybe you can't say no or delegate work to other people.

Regardless of what your life is like today, if you can manage your time and energy to implement the ideas and suggestions in this chapter, things you never thought were possible will begin to happen.

Final Thoughts

Please know that it is no small feat to go after what you want and be responsible for working, running a home, and if you have children, raising the children. I know for me, my career didn't really take off until my son was older.

It's normal to feel frustrated about having no time or energy and wanting to follow a dream. Frustration is a positive sign that says "you need to follow your destiny." If you were satisfied, you would stay the way you are.

The next time you are tempted to beat yourself up over the fact that you are stuck and can't make a dream come true, remember it is almost impossible to accomplish a goal when all your time is spent doing low-level activities.

Be patient and kind to yourself. Beating yourself up for things you cannot control doesn't do you any good. Remember, nothing stays the same and eventually your situation will change.

Finally, when you are discouraged and feel that it's too late or too difficult to get what you really want, remember this: a dream is a beginning. So, your age or situation doesn't matter—you are just getting started.

Sandra's Success Secrets

You are closer than you think.

Time doesn't matter
when you are doing something you love.

The more you value yourself,
the more you value your time.

11

Conquer Stress

*S*tress can keep you from living the life you were meant to live because when stress consumes you, it becomes your focus. And the more you focus on stress, the worse it gets.

Stress can negatively affect four areas of your life: your relationships, your job, your personal life, or your finances. If two or more areas of your life are affected by stress at the same time, it feels as if you are being eaten alive by a monster.

You must find a way to conquer your stress. If you don't, it will squash every ounce of joy and happiness from you and leave you depleted, exhausted, and defeated. Your goal: to tame the stress monster.

Ten Steps to Conquer Your Stress

These ten steps are not easy to do because they are not what you are used to. It will take patience and attention for you to make these a part of your daily life. They work though, trust me!

1. Know your stressors.

2. Honor your season.

3. Plan for a change of season.

4. Put yourself in the equation.

5. Unplug.

6. Little matters.

7. Positive ain't always positive.

8. Talk nice to yourself.

9. Have a sense of purpose.

10. Create a ritual for renewal.

Step 1: Know Your Stressors

A great way to begin conquering your stress is to think about and acknowledge what is stressful to you. To do that, I have created a three-part exercise for you to complete.

You have already done this type of exercise in chapter six, "How to Handle Emotions." Feel free to skip step 1 in this chapter if you learned how to control your thoughts in chapter six.

Part A: What is stressful?

Let's look at what is stressful to you. Grab your workbook and go to the section for this chapter, "How to Conquer Stress." Copy the three related pages from the appendix for this exercise, "What Is Stressful," "I Can Control These Stressors," and "I Cannot Control These Stressors."

Please check off what is causing you stress either at home or at work, from the following list of what is stressful:

What Is Stressful

_____Money

_____Lack of energy

_____Gas prices

_____Slackers at work

_____Worry

_____Family issues

_____Traffic

_____Children

_____Tragedies

_____Not enough time

_____Managers

_____School

_____Commute to work

_____Clients

_____World events

_____Workload

_____Being a single parent

_____Life in general

_____Health

_____Relationships

_____Supervisor

_____Teenagers

_____Gray hair

_____Employees

_____Housework

_____Weight

_____Parents

_____Pets

_____The unknown

_____Clutter

_____Stress

_____Ex-spouse

_____Being disorganized

_____Lack of time

_____Empty nest

_____Housework

_____Caring for aging parents

_____Needing a new car

_____Coworkers

_____Negative people

_____Aging

_____HR reform

_____Work environment

_____Illness

_____Not enough women

_____Not enough men

_____Limited resources

It is clear to see that life can be really challenging! These stressors affect so many people, particularly women. Just to let you know, this list came from attendees at my stress seminars. Now that you know what is stressful, let's take a look at what you can and cannot control.

Part B: What stressors can you control?

Looking at your list of what is stressful to you, which ones would you say you can control? Please write them down and insert the page into your workbook.

> **I Can Control These Stressors**
>
> _____
>
> _____
>
> _____

Part C: What stressors can't you control?

Now, look at your list of what is stressful to you again, and write down the ones that you think you cannot control?

> **I Cannot Control These Stressors**
>
> _____
>
> _____
>
> _____

Here is what is stressing you out: when you try to control what is stressing you out! It's impossible! And, the harder you try, the worse it gets! It's called the stress of stress.

The teaching point here is that you must stop thinking about the stress long enough to figure out a solution. And, if there is no solution, you must figure out a way to cope with the stress. Remember, the more you focus ON the stress, the bigger the stress monster gets.

Here is how to find a solution. Something comes up. Ask yourself, "Is this something I can or cannot control?" If the answer is "Yes, I can control it," try. If the answer is "No, I can't control it," ask yourself, "What can I control?" Your answer, "My response."

Now you say to yourself, "I have three choices. I can accept it, change it, or leave it." Pick one, and then move on. Read chapter six, "How to Handle Emotions," for more information on how to control your thoughts and create empowered thinking.

The bottom line to step 1: It's not what happens to you that matters, it's your response to what happens to you that matters.

Step 2: Honor Your Season

I want to tell you about a woman I met while I was doing a stress and balance workshop in Honolulu. All through my workshop, she cried. During lunch she approached me and said, "I hate my mother."

I said, "OK." She said, "No, you don't understand, I hate my mother and she lives with me and my husband!" So I suggested, "Kick her out if you hate her." "No," she replied, "In my culture you take care of your parents until they die. We don't put our parents in nursing homes."

Then I asked her, "What do you say to yourself when you wake up in the morning?"

Every morning I say, "I hate my mother!"

I pulled a Dr. Phil and asked her, "How's that working for you?"

"Not good," she said. "In fact, all I do is cry and I can't seem to stop crying about it."

I explained to her and the others at my workshop that life is like seasons. When you're at a season in your life where you have aging parents and you must care for them, choose to honor that choice by accepting your choice.

When you do not accept your choices, you end up with low energy, no motivation, and lots of stress. I am not saying she should change her feelings about her mother, but rather, honor her choice of care giving for her mother.

Months passed and one day I received an e-mail from the woman in my workshop. In it she said, "The only time I cry now is when I visit my mother at the cemetery." You see, seasons changed and her mother did pass away like nature intended.

Now, she can look herself in the mirror and know she honored her choice of care giving for her mother. This woman also role-modeled to her young daughter the value of family and doing the right thing.

This example can lend itself to just about any work or family situation you can think of. Take your weight, for instance. When you weigh what you weigh but you constantly call yourself fat and lazy, those thoughts and words disempower and dishonor you.

Accept your body just as it is today. Regardless of what you weigh, always honor where you are at today. In other words, change things in a positive way by moving toward what you want rather than hating what you already have.

The bottom line to step 2: Accept your choices as they are today.

Step 3: Plan for a Change of Season

One day I picked up a magazine and read a four-page interview about a successful businesswoman who had her own makeup line and designed beautiful porcelain dolls. The last question the interviewer asked this successful woman was, "How do you feel about aging?"

She replied, "Well, if you have financial security, you are proud of what you've done, and you have your health, aging is not too bad." When I read that it practically knocked me over.

That is exactly what it means to plan for a change of season: plan today for your tomorrow. You must put money aside each month for your future. You must stay in touch with what you love and not just do for others, and you must stay healthy by staying happy.

Your life happens in seasons. One season may be college. The next season might be marriage, then possibly children. The next season might be a career change. Taking care of aging parents or having grown children return home may be your next season.

Whatever you are going through today will eventually change. If you feel stressed out and stuck, your situation can feel like it will last forever. The good news is that your tomorrow can be more exciting than today.

The bottom line to step 3: You can do everything you want to do, just not in the same season.

Step 4: Put Yourself in the Equation

Stress problems arise when you have something you want to do but feel you can't because you are too busy doing for others. In other words, you end up leaving yourself out of your own life.

You must put yourself in the equation. When was the last time you did something just for you? Asked for some help cooking dinner? Said no to a party invitation because you needed time alone?

When you are always doing for others you do not have the time or energy to do something that would bring you happiness. Continually denying yourself those activities that can renew your spirit will eventually deplete your inner energy source. And that is like driving your car on empty.

Look closely at your reasons to wait. Are you going to wait to do something you want to do until your kids are grown, or when you lose ten pounds, or when you will have enough time?

And if and when you do participate in activities that you enjoy, don't feel guilty about it. Look at it this way, when you do something just for you, others benefit from your happiness.

The bottom line to step 4: Do as much for yourself as you do for others and treat yourself as well as you treat your family.

Step 5: Unplug

One of the most-asked questions I get after a seminar is this: "Sandra, where do you get all your energy?" The answer is "I unplug." Meaning, when I work I'm plugged in, and when I have a small window of time, I totally unplug.

Here's an example. When I fly home after a speaking engagement, I will sit and stare at a screw on the back of the airline seat in front of me. I am not thinking, speaking, or creating anything. Just the opposite—I'm unplugged. Mentally I am somewhere else, focusing on beautiful images.

You can compare your busy life to a battery-operated radio that is left on High all the time. Eventually the battery goes dead. Well, so do you. When you always do for others and never take the time to renew, refresh, and replenish, you burn out.

The usual argument I hear for why you don't unplug is either lack of time or lack of money. Unplugging does not mean you need to take a three-week vacation in the Bahamas. I am talking about small increments of time on a regular basis.

Find your own way to unplug. It could be walking, reading, dancing, talking, or meditating. It doesn't have to cost a dime and can take as little as three minutes. It's the intent and clarity of focus that creates the end result of feeling renewed, refreshed, and replenished.

The bottom line to step 5: The opposite of doing is not doing. You must find small moments in time to do nothing.

Step 6: Little Matters

If I could leave you with one tip that can dramatically change your life, it is that little matters. This concept of little matters came up in chapter ten, "How to Find Time," and it will help you conquer stress as well.

Here is what creates stress:

- The pressure of too much to do and not enough time to get it all done.

- Constantly doing stuff, but feeling you're not getting anywhere.

- Getting everything done for work and home, but not doing anything for you.

The way you handle the stress of having too much to do is to break everything into smaller pieces. Whether it's a report you are doing at work, saving money, going back to college, or journaling before you go to bed. You do have time, except you only have a small window of time.

The bottom line for step 6: Pursue the things you love and do them in small chunks of time.

Step 7: Positive Ain't Always Positive

What do you need to be doing, but aren't, because you are waiting for your attitude to change? For example, will you walk when you feel motivated? You will start saving money when you feel better about investing? You will say no to someone when you feel empowered?

Don't wait to do what you need to do, just do it. You don't need to feel like walking, just go for a walk. You don't need to feel comfortable about investing, just throw $10 in a purple plastic bucket every Friday night. You don't need to feel empowered to tell someone no, just say no.

To use me as an example, I couldn't worry if I liked writing this book or not, it just had to be done because of my passion: to help people discover their purpose and destiny.

In other words, the thought of sitting twelve hours a day didn't excite me, but the more I thought about the possibility of this book helping you fulfill your potential, the more excited I got.

I recommend you read Barbara Sher's book *I Could Do Anything*

If I Only Knew What It Was. She is the person I give credit to for presenting a no-nonsense approach to attitude. She also has a great Web site, barbarasher.com, and other great books.

The bottom line to step 7: Do what you need to do, whether you like it or not, because the benefits of doing it are greater than the benefits of not doing it.

Step 8: Talk Nice to Yourself

What do you say to yourself when you try something and it doesn't work out? Do you say "It failed" or "I failed"? "It failed" means you did something, it didn't work out, and you will try again. "I failed" means you did something, it didn't work out, and you blame *yourself* that it failed.

If you attempt to try something new and it fails, and your response is, "What is wrong with me?" it makes you doubt your intelligence and/or ability. To avoid this painful state of self-doubt, you will avoid taking risks or trying new things.

Try this instead. When you encounter a challenge, tell yourself that you have the ability to problem solve. Use positive self-talk and know that you will reach your goal. Failing at something does not make you a failure; it just means you need another strategy.

Another helpful idea is to create the "Magic Three" list. At the end of your day, list three things you have accomplished. You do this to help you focus on what you are accomplishing, rather than focusing on what isn't done. When you always focus on what isn't done, you can end up feeling drained and depleted.

As simple as this exercise sounds, you would be surprised at how many people discount or minimize what or how much they actually do in a day. And, when you start keeping track, you begin to see why you are so tired and stressed out. The more you do this exercise, the more you see what you are accomplishing. Make several copies of the appropriate page from the appendix and keep it in your workbook, filling it out each evening.

The Magic Three

Three things I accomplished today:

1. _____

2. _____

3. _____

A "Golden Five" list works well, too, to help you become more supportive and loving toward yourself. On this list, list five things you like about yourself. Often we are quick to focus on our negatives, so let's focus on the positives. Also, acknowledging what you like about yourself helps you uncover and embrace your true authentic self.

The Golden Five

Five things I like about myself:

1. _____

2. _____

3. _____

4. _____

5. _____

Finally, be watchful for your inner critic, that negative and critical voice inside your head. As you learned in chapter five, you must silence the Critic's voice and diminish its power by talking back to it; always override its negative comments.

The bottom line to step 8: If you think bad thoughts about yourself, you will feel bad about yourself—you will say negative things about yourself, and then give up.

Step 9: Have a Sense of Purpose

Tango dancing is a very sensuous dance. When the couple moves to the rhythm of the music, they are totally in tune with one another as they focus on the purpose of that moment—to tango.

When you watch them dance, you will see expressions of intensity and excitement as they glide around the dance floor. They are inches from each other as they move in every direction. Each turn is as if it were a surprise.

They love the tango because it involves them in something much deeper than taking steps on a dance floor; the dance evokes and immerses them in feelings of joy and love. And that joy and love is shared and exchanged with their partner.

This, to me, is purpose. It is deep joy and love inside your soul that radiates out to others. It is intensity and excitement. It is doing something you have done before, but with surprise. It is face-to-face, and free to move. It can happen anywhere and anytime.

Don't wait for your purpose to show up to be inspired, motivated, and energized. Jump into life. Wake up as if you have had a cold shower. Get up everyday knowing you are living your purpose.

Remind yourself, "Everything I do today is part of who I am becoming. My purpose for right now is to be in this place, at this time, doing exactly what I am doing." Then, like the tango dancers, enjoy every moment of the dance.

I want to make one more point about having a sense of purpose. Everyone who meets you, meets you for a purpose. In other words, you do have a role of purpose in relation to other people.

Let me explain. I had just finished a speaking engagement, jumped into my rental car, and headed for the freeway. As I was driving, I realized I was totally lost. While waiting at a red light, I looked over at the car in the next lane.

This guy looked over at me and yelled out, "Are you OK?"

I said, "No, I'm lost and I need Highway 102."

"Keep driving," he said. "I'm not from around here either, but

I'll find out where 102 is and I'll be back and help you find it."

Off he went, and I kept driving. About nine blocks later, he pulled alongside my car and gestured for me to follow him. We snaked our way up and down streets for about three miles. As I looked ahead, I saw a big green sign that read Highway 102.

As we approached the highway entrance, he stuck his hand out his car window and pointed to my freeway onramp. As I drove in the direction he pointed, I saw him drive off in the opposite direction, never to see him again.

After driving on Highway 102 for about ten minutes, I began to cry. I realized that his purpose that day was to be a guardian angel for me. He was exactly where he was supposed to be because I needed him.

That's what I call a magical moment and you have hundreds of magical moments just like that. You have been a guardian angel for someone, too, but most of the time you just don't know it. Just because you can't see your purpose, doesn't mean it's not there.

For more discussion on finding your purpose, read chapter two, "How to Ignite Energy."

The bottom line to step 9: Your life's purpose is shown to you in your everyday life and is well hidden in your love, joy, and excitement.

Step 10: Create a Ritual for Renewal

A ritual for renewal is any activity you do on a regular and consistent basis as part of your daily schedule for the purpose of renewing, refreshing, and replenishing your spirit. This is the best way to lower stress!

You must choose an activity you can enjoy and stick with. Even on your busiest day, you've got to find a small increment of time to renew. If money is an issue, you must find an activity that doesn't cost a dime. And, you must enjoy the activity without feeling guilty!

So, what can you come up with? Why don't you copy the sheet

named "Renewal Activities" from the appendix, grab your workbook, and brainstorm some ideas. Think about and write down activities you can do to renew your spirit that will have special meaning to you.

Here are some ideas: a short walk, sitting on your bed meditating, coffee at Starbucks, spending time with your cat, going online and checking out a trip to France, calling your best friend, tea in a pretty cup, a bath, or reading your journal.

Renewal Activities

_____

_____

_____

_____

How did that go for you? If it was easy, great, you are good to go. If it was hard to do, here are some extra tips:

- A renewal activity is any activity you feel personally connected to.

- Pick any activity and get going; you can always change your mind.

- An activity doesn't mean you have to do something. Your activity can be to do nothing; like being alone for twenty minutes.

Now that you have brainstormed renewal activities, pick one from your list to start with. I am going to ask you if you would be willing to commit to a one-month agreement to do your renewal activity.

If you answered yes, then I have a contract for you to sign! This is optional, of course; however, my intent is to help you to get motivated and committed to making this happen. You can copy the contract from the appendix and insert it in your workbook in chapter eleven.

Renewal Activity Commitment Contract

I (name)_____,
am committed to my renewal activity. I will begin
(list your activity)_____
on (date)_____.
I will do my activity (number of times) _____per week
for one month.

Signed: _____

Date:_____

I hope this exercise feels like a small step to you. In others words, just do one activity a couple of times a week for one month. If you can keep up with the program, I promise you will begin to feel less stress.

After a month, I recommend you renew your contract. Your goal is to make certain that you always include activities in your schedule that you do just for you for the purpose of renewing your spirit.

If you stop doing your renewal activity because you feel guilty for taking time for yourself, continue the activity and stop the guilt. Your body and soul will know that you respect them when you care for them.

Guilt and neglect of one's self sends a clear message to your subconscious that you don't matter. And you do matter! So, fight your own negative thinking by continuing your renewal activity.

If other people try to get you to stop doing stuff just for you and you cave in, you send them the message that you don't respect yourself. Respect yourself by standing up for yourself. Remember, people respect people who respect themselves.

The bottom line to step 10: Every day you must do something just for you.

Chapter Recap

If you can master and use these ten steps in your daily life, you will develop great mental and emotional inner strength. Being strong internally is the best way to conquer stress. Let's go over these steps one more time.

Acknowledging and finding solutions to overcome your "stressors" will lower your stress. That's because when you focus on something you can control, it empowers you. Remember, empowerment is about choice.

"Honor your season" means accept your choices and when you're ready to change, you will. Accept your weight, your finances, your job, and your current living situation. Feeling a sense of acceptance, rather than being angry or victimized, can energize and motivate you to change your situation.

"Plan for a change of season" reminds you that nothing stays the same. People die, children grow up and leave home, and friendships dissolve. Prepare yourself by doing for yourself along with doing for others. It's when we put everyone else before us that we end up angry, lonely, and full of regret.

When we do for others and leave ourselves out of the "equation," it is the quickest way to feel depleted and drained. Every day, in your busy schedule, do something just for you. And never feel guilty for being good at self-care and self-respect.

It's time to balance doing with not doing. "Unplug" means you intentionally do something that turns you off even for as little as three minutes. You must recharge or you will burn out. This is a cause-and-effect action of life.

My top tip for less stress is "little matters." Every time you take one small step toward your goal, you create energy. Not taking a small step makes you feel stuck and that creates stress. Move forward by breaking big steps into small steps because little matters.

"Positive ain't always positive" means you don't have to like what you need to do, you just need to do it. The positive benefits of accomplishing something, whether you want to do it or not, far outweigh giving into a negative feeling and not doing what it is you know you need to do.

Your thoughts and how to "talk" to yourself affect everything you do. Override your negative internal language with positive language by replacing it in the moment. Remember, what you put thought to grows.

Your life's "purpose" is found in everything you do. You are at the exact place you need to be, doing just what you need to be doing, and becoming the person you were meant to be.

Lastly, a "ritual for renewal" means doing something just for you. By continuously renewing your spirit, you create an unlimited supply of inner strength that will help you get what you really want in life—without the guilt.

Sandra's Success Secrets

Stress ages you and happiness keeps you young.

Most people have no invisible means of support.

*Stress is when you try to control the
very thing that is stressing you out.*

Summary

Well, I've said everything I wanted to say. I hope you benefited from spending time with this book. I want to close by leaving you with a powerful message from Max Steingart.

Success is Within You

How things look on the outside of you always depends on
how things are on the inside of you.

Your thoughts have brought you to where you are today.
Your actions always mirror your thoughts.
Take a good look at where you are and what you're doing,
and you can understand what you've been thinking.
Your mind is your true essence.

Your behavior is the perpetual revealing of yourself.
What you do, tells everyone who and what you are.

Change your thoughts and you can change your position in life.
You can start this process at any time.
Why not start today?

©2006 by Max Steingart

Appendix

Get What You Really Want
—WORKBOOK—

The pages that follow can be copied and inserted into your *Get What You Really Want* Workbook. Each page is listed under the appropriate chapter.

A three-ring binder will be a great place for you to work on all of the questions and exercises presented in each chapter. Make and label a section for each chapter, and then photocopy the work pages from this appendix to insert in each section. You may want to insert some blank pages into each section for your notes as well.

Your *Get What You Really Want* Workbook will help you stay focused on what you want, keep your momentum going, and record and review how much you have grown.

Workbook Contents

Self-Knowledge Questionnaire

Yes	No	
___	___	I feel I have too much stress in my life.
___	___	I sleep too much or not enough.
___	___	I overeat or do not eat enough.
___	___	I look to others for approval.
___	___	I constantly focus on things I cannot control.
___	___	I feel stuck in my comfort zone.
___	___	I wish I could control my emotions.
___	___	Enough is never enough for me.
___	___	I avoid conflict.
___	___	I wish I could stop being a perfectionist.
___	___	I take forever to make a decision because I lack confidence.
___	___	I make a decision, and then replay my decision with regret.
___	___	After an argument, I find it difficult to move on.
___	___	I feel selfish when I ask for what I want.
___	___	I feel an overwhelming sense of failure.
___	___	I lack energy.
___	___	I lack motivation.
___	___	I stay with someone I no longer love.
___	___	I constantly second-guess myself.

Yes	No	
___	___	I distract myself from my feelings by staying busy.
___	___	I believe you should settle for what you already have.
___	___	I take everything personally.
___	___	I get stressed out when I procrastinate.
___	___	I have physical clutter but feel unable to get rid of it.
___	___	I hate my job but keep working there.
___	___	I lose energy just thinking about an upcoming project.
___	___	I hate the way my body looks.
___	___	I can still hear the voice of my critical mother or father.
___	___	I feel I lack time to do something just for me.
___	___	I worry a lot.
___	___	I feel lonely.
___	___	I feel I lack emotional support.
___	___	I am concerned with my finances.
___	___	I engage in negative self-talk.
___	___	It is hard to establish and maintain healthy relationships.
___	___	I get embarrassed and/or disregard compliments.
___	___	I hate getting older.
___	___	I feel guilty when I ask for what I want or need.
___	___	I am unable to deal with my fears.
___	___	I blame myself when things go wrong.

Acquiring Self-Empowering Beliefs

On the left side, list the statements you recorded with a yes on the Self-Knowledge Questionnaire. Then, on the right side, rewrite each negative self-limiting belief into a positive self-empowering belief.

Negative Self-Limiting Beliefs   **Positive Self-Empowering Beliefs**

_____   _____

_____   _____

_____   _____

_____   _____

_____   _____

_____   _____

_____   _____

_____   _____

_____   _____

_____   _____

_____   _____

_____   _____

_____   _____

_____   _____

_____   _____

Identifying Limitations

What is my belief?

_____

_____

_____

_____

Is it holding me back?

_____

_____

_____

_____

How?

_____

_____

_____

_____

What I Want to Have

_____

_____

_____

_____

_____

_____

_____

_____

_____

_____

_____

_____

_____

_____

_____

_____

_____

Becoming Who I Need to Be

I want this:

_____

_____

_____

_____

BE

_____

_____

_____

_____

DO

_____

_____

_____

_____

HAVE

_____

_____

_____

_____

My Life Today

I do

_____

_____

_____

_____

_____

_____

_____

_____

I want to do

_____

_____

_____

_____

_____

_____

_____

_____

My Purpose and Passion

Date it	Choose it	Do it	Feel it

My Future Life If Nothing Changes

1. Who will I become in five years if I stay the same?

_____

_____

2. Where will I be working in five years if things stay the same?

_____

_____

3. How much money will I be earning in five years if things stay the same?

_____

_____

4. Where will I be living in five years if things stay the same?

_____

_____

5. Who will I be in love with in five years if things stay the same?

_____

_____

6. What will I be like in five years if things stay the same?

_____

_____

7. What will I look like in five years if things stay the same?

_____

_____

8. What do I think I won't be doing in five years but wish I were?

_____

_____

My Present Life

1. What negative thoughts, beliefs, and habits are keeping me from my ideal life?

_____

_____

_____

2. Which of those am I able to change?

_____

_____

_____

3. Which of those am I unable to change?

_____

_____

_____

4. Which thoughts, beliefs, and attitudes can I accept that I cannot control or change?

_____

_____

_____

My Commitment to Change

1. What do you want to change?

_____

_____

_____

_____

_____

_____

2. What is your reason to change?

_____

_____

_____

_____

_____

_____

3. How are you going to do that?

_____

_____

_____

_____

_____

_____

My Awesome Life in Five Years

1. Who will I become in five years?

_____

_____

2. Where will I be working in five years?

_____

_____

3. How much money will I be earning in five years?

_____

_____

4. Where will I be living in five years?

_____

_____

5. Who will I be in love with in five years?

_____

_____

6. What will I be like in five years?

_____

_____

7. What will I look like in five years?

_____

_____

8. What will I be doing in five years that I am most proud of?

_____

_____

9. When will I start creating my new future?

_____

_____

10. How will I begin creating my new future?

_____

_____

My Needs

(Write in activity)   *(Check which need applies)*

What I do   **Challenge**   **Variety**   **Control**   **Security**

_____   _____

_____   _____

_____   _____

_____   _____

_____   _____

_____   _____

_____   _____

_____   _____

_____   _____

_____   _____

_____   _____

_____   _____

Core Belief Questionnaire

Yes No

___ ___ Do you believe you're *worthy* of success?

___ ___ Do you *expect* to have a great life?

___ ___ Do you believe you can *change?*

___ ___ Do you believe you have *what it takes* to succeed?

___ ___ Do you believe you *deserve* what you want?

___ ___ Do you believe you are *responsible* for your own life?

Communication: My Inner Critic

1. Do you feel you have an inner critic?

_____

_____

2. If you answered yes, what does it say to you?

_____

_____

3. Does it get worse under certain conditions?

_____

_____

4. What are those conditions?

_____

_____

5. When you listen to your inner critic, whose voice are you hearing?

_____

_____

6. When you decide to change or accomplish something outside of your comfort zone, what does your inner critic say?

_____

_____

7. Are you hearing positive or negative comments?

_____

_____

8. Does your inner critic keep you stuck?

_____

_____

Who Am I?

What words come to mind when you think of you?
Please write them down.

_____

_____

_____

_____

_____

_____

_____

_____

_____

_____

_____

_____

_____

How Others See Me

Find a partner. This exercise works best if you do not know one another. Share information about yourself for five minutes, then allow your partner to share information about himself or herself for five minutes.

Write down one word to describe how you see yourself and write down one word to describe your partner. Have your partner do the same thing. Don't look at each other's notes.

Compare what you wrote with your partner. For some of you, the words you wrote down will match your partner's words exactly, and for others your words may be totally different.

"People think I am _____, and I think I am_____"

_____

_____

_____

_____

_____

_____

_____

_____

_____

Things I Can't Control/My Stressors

_____

_____

_____

_____

_____

_____

_____

_____

_____

_____

_____

_____

_____

_____

_____

_____

_____

_____

_____

Things I Can Control

_____

_____

_____

_____

_____

_____

_____

_____

_____

_____

_____

_____

_____

_____

_____

_____

_____

_____

_____

_____

Assertiveness Script

_____

_____

_____

_____

_____

_____

_____

_____

_____

_____

_____

_____

_____

_____

_____

_____

_____

_____

_____

What Do I Fear?

_____

_____

_____

_____

_____

_____

_____

_____

_____

_____

_____

_____

_____

_____

_____

_____

_____

_____

My Negative Labels

I tell myself that I am:

_____

_____

_____

_____

_____

_____

_____

_____

_____

_____

_____

_____

_____

_____

_____

_____

_____

_____

_____

My Positive Labels

I am:

_____

_____

_____

_____

_____

_____

_____

_____

_____

_____

_____

_____

_____

_____

_____

_____

_____

_____

Internal and External Barriers to Motivation

Think of what you want. What is it that you want?
Do you want to start a business, end a relationship,
change jobs, or lose weight? Write down your answer.

My goal, desire, or dream:

_____

_____

_____

_____

_____

Think of what your barriers might
be to getting what you want.

My barriers to getting what I really want:

_____

_____

_____

_____

_____

Now that you see your goal and barriers written down,
what do you think? Can you see how motivation is not the
answer to accomplishing your goal? The way you accomplish
your goal is to first overcome your barriers.

WHAT YOU WANT

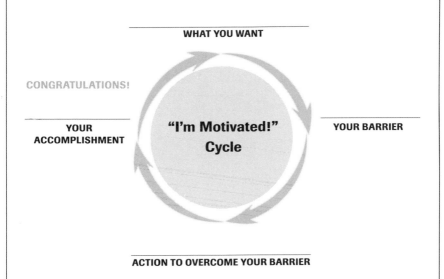

CONGRATULATIONS!

YOUR
ACCOMPLISHMENT

"I'm Motivated!"
Cycle

YOUR BARRIER

ACTION TO OVERCOME YOUR BARRIER

Thoughts, Beliefs, and Activities I Want to Quit/Start Doing

Thoughts, beliefs, and activities I want to *quit* doing:

_____

_____

_____

_____

_____

_____

Thoughts, beliefs, and activities I want to *start* doing:

_____

_____

_____

_____

_____

_____

_____

What My Home Says About Me

_____

_____

_____

Now, would you say that your home expresses who you really are?

_____

If yes, why?

_____

If no, why?

_____

Here are more questions about the
individual rooms in your house:

My bedroom feels

_____

My kitchen feels

_____

My living room feels

_____

My bathroom feels

_____

Notes:

_____

_____

_____

Clear Clutter Worksheet

Room:

_____

Mini Area #1   **Mini Area #2**   **Mini Area #3**

_____

☐ Completed!   ☐ Completed!   ☐ Completed!

Mini Area #4   **Mini Area #5**   **Mini Area #6**

_____

☐ Completed!   ☐ Completed!   ☐ Completed!

Energy Drainers

These take away your energy:

___	Lack of time	___	Working at a job I hate
___	Negativity	___	Conflict and confrontation
___	Self-doubt	___	Toxic relationships
___	Lack of direction	___	Caring for aging parents
___	An inability to say "no"	___	Lack of faith
___	Guilt	___	Weight issues
___	Victim mentality	___	Always tired
___	Feel I have no choices	___	Can't sleep well at night
___	Too many low-level activities like housework and chores	___	Too old
___	Stress	___	Inconsiderate people
___	Feeling I'm never good enough	___	Procrastination
___	Judgmental self-labeling like stupid, selfish, or lazy	___	Lack of belief
___	Living up to others' standards	___	Old bad habits
___	Lack of self-respect, self-value, or self-worth	___	Worry
___	Poor health	___	Lack of education
___	Always doing for others and never for myself	___	Can't stop thinking about things and take action
___	Lack of money	___	Lack of self-acceptance
___	Too concerned about what others think of me	___	Change
___	Loneliness	___	Anger
___	Fear of failure or fear of success	___	Insecurity
		___	Unhealthy habits
		___	Lack of trust

Energy Boosters

These add to your energy:

___ When I get stuff done

___ Hopefulness

___ Recognition

___ Rewards

___ Seeing others happy

___ Feeling good about myself

___ Having time off from work

___ Balance

___ Contentment

___ Joy

___ Success: Financial, occupational, relational, personal

___ Having fun

___ Health

___ Losing weight

___ Being with family and/or friends

___ Good food

___ Security

___ Intimacy with my partner

___ Being creative

___ Alone time

___ Overcoming an obstacle

___ Love

___ Meditating or praying

___ Journaling

___ Looking in the mirror and liking what I see

___ Participating in hobbies I enjoy

___ Living in a space that feels clean and organized

___ Happiness

___ Feeling a divine connection to a higher power

___ Loving myself unconditionally

___ Learning new things

___ Climbing the corporate ladder

___ Control

___ Children

___ Self-fulfillment

___ A retirement plan

___ Encouraging other people

___ Making good choices

___ Working at a job I love

___ Having a dream

___ Being in nature

___ Travel

___ Better family relationships

___ Doing something good that helps others

___ Fulfilling my destiny

___ Money

___ Goals

___ Pets

___ Knowing my purpose in life

___ Shopping

___ Humor and laughter

___ Passion

___ Getting remarried

___ Optimism

___ Music

My Daily Activities

_____

_____

_____

_____

_____

_____

_____

_____

_____

_____

_____

_____

_____

_____

_____

_____

_____

_____

_____

_____

What Is Stressful?

___ Money	___ Employees
___ Lack of energy	___ Housework
___ Gas prices	___ Weight
___ Slackers at work	___ Parents
___ Worry	___ Pets
___ Family issues	___ The unknown
___ Traffic	___ Clutter
___ Children	___ Stress
___ Tragedies	___ Ex-spouse
___ Not enough time	___ Being disorganized
___ Managers	___ Lack of time
___ School	___ Empty nest
___ Commute to work	___ Housework
___ Clients	___ Caring for aging parents
___ World events	___ Needing a new car
___ Workload	___ Coworkers
___ Being a single parent	___ Negative people
___ Life in general	___ Aging
___ Health	___ HR reform
___ Relationships	___ Work environment
___ Health	___ Illness
___ Supervisor	___ Not enough women
___ Teenagers	___ Not enough men
___ Gray hair	___ Limited resources

I Can Control These Stressors

_____

_____

_____

_____

_____

_____

_____

_____

_____

_____

_____

_____

_____

I Cannot Control These Stressors

_____

_____

_____

_____

_____

_____

_____

_____

_____

_____

_____

_____

_____

_____

The Magic Three

Three things I accomplished today:

1. _____

2. _____

3. _____

Three things I accomplished today:

1. _____

2. _____

3. _____

Three things I accomplished today:

1. _____

2. _____

3. _____

Three things I accomplished today:

1. _____

2. _____

3. _____

The Golden Five

Five things I like about myself:

1. _____

2. _____

3. _____

4. _____

5. _____

Renewal Activities

_____

_____

_____

_____

_____

_____

_____

_____

_____

_____

_____

_____

_____

_____

_____

_____

_____

_____

_____

_____

Renewal Activity Commitment Contract

I (name)_____,

am committed to my renewal activity. I will begin (list your activity)

_____

on (date) _____.

I will do my activity (number of times)_____ per week for one

month.

        Signed:_____

        Date:_____

Recommended Reading

These are my favorites. There is a mix of business, health, and spiritual. Finding a good book is like finding a good friend.

Anderson, Nancy. *Work with Passion: How to Do What You Love for a Living*, New World Library, 1995.

Angelou, Maya. *Still I Rise*, Random House, 2001.

Batmanghelidj, F. *Your Body's Many Cries for Water*, Global Health Solutions, 1995.

Cameron, Julia. *The Artist's Way: A Spiritual Path to Higher Creativity*, Putnam Publishing, 1992.

Campbell, Joseph and David Kudler. *Pathways to Bliss: Mythology and Personal Transformation*, New World Library, 2004.

Carr-Ruffino, Norma. *The Promotable Woman*, Career Press, 1997.

Carter, Karen Rauch. *Move Your Stuff, Change Your Life: How to Use Feng Shui to Get Love, Money, Respect, and Happiness*, Simon & Schuster, 2000.

Chopra, Deepak. *Quantum Healing: Exploring the Frontiers of Mind/Body Medicine*, Bantam Books, 1989.

Cook, Sunny Kobe. *Common Things Uncommon Ways*, Achievement Dynamics, 2002.

Covey, Stephen R. *The 7 Habits of Highly Effective People*, Fireside, 1990.

Dyer, Wayne W. *Manifest Your Destiny*, HarperTorch, 1999.

Dyer, Wayne W. *The Power of Intention*, Hay House, 2004.

Edwards, Paul and Sarah Edwards. *Finding Your Perfect Work: The New Career Guide to Making a Living, Creating a Life*, Tarcher/Putman Books, 1996.

Gavin, Bill. *No White at Night*, Riverhead, 2004.

Goleman, Daniel. *Emotional Intelligence*, Bantam Books, 1997.

Hill, Napoleon. *Think and Grow Rich*, Fawcett Books, 1990.

Hurley Kathleen and Theodore Dobson. *My Best Self: Using the Enneagram to Free the Soul*, HarperCollins Publishers, 1993.

Kingston, Karen. *Creating Sacred Space with Feng Shui*, Broadway Books, 1997.

McGraw, Phillip C. *Self Matters: Creating Your Life from the Inside Out*, Simon & Schuster, 2001.

Myss, Caroline. *Anatomy of the Spirit: The Seven Stages of Power and Healing*, Harmony, 1996.

Orman, Suze. *9 Steps to Financial Freedom: Practical and Spiritual Steps So You Can Stop Worrying*, Three Rivers Press, 2006.

Peale, Norman Vincent. *The Power of Positive Thinking*, Ballantine Books, 1996.

Poynter, Dan. *The Self-Publishing Manual: How to Write, Print, and Sell Your Own Book*, Para Publishing, 2003.

Reeves, Nancy. *I'd Say Yes, God If I Knew What You Wanted*, Northstone Publishing, 2001.

Roffer, Robin Fisher. *Make a Name for Yourself: Eight Steps Every Woman Needs to Create a Personal Brand Strategy for Success*, Broadway Books, 2000.

Ross, Ruth. *Prospering Woman: A Complete Guide to Achieving the Full, Abundant Life*, Whatever Publishing, 1982.

SantoPietro, Nancy. *Feng Shui: Harmony by Design*, Perigee Book, 1996.

Seligman, Martin E. P. *Learned Optimism: How to Change Your Mind and Your Life*, Pocket Books, 1998.

Sher, Barbara. *I Could Do Anything If I Only Knew What It Was: How to Discover What You Really Want and How to Get It*, Dell Publishing, 1994.

Smith, Hyrum. *What Matters Most*, Simon & Schuster, 2000.

Tieger, Paul D. and Barbara Barron-Tieger. *Do What You Are: Discover the Perfect Career for You Through the Secrets of Personality Type*, Little, Brown & Company, 1995.

Tolle, Eckhart. *The Power of Now: A Guide to Spiritual Enlightenment*, New World Library, 1999.

Tracy, Brian. *Maximum Achievement*, Simon & Schuster, 1990.

Tracy, Brian. *Focal Point*, AMACOM Books, 2002.

Ventus-Darks, Kimberly. *If I'm So Special, Why Do I Feel Ordinary?* (Audio CD), Rockhurst University Continuing Education Press, 2003.

Walters, Dottie and Lilly Walters. *Speak and Grow Rich*, Prentice Hall, 1997.

Zukav, Gary. *The Seat of the Soul*, Simon & Schuster, 1990.

Author's Page

Now that you've read the book, was it helpful? We would love to hear from you about how you are using the information and how you have benefited from this book.

Just e-mail us your thoughts and your testimonial could appear on our Web site or in the next book. Don't worry, your contact information will never, ever be posted publicly.

We are extending a personal invitation for you to join the Aspire family. You simply go to the Aspire Seminars Web site and enter your contact information. You will have access to inspirational messages, great tips, and ideas that will enrich your life. Again, your contact information will not be shared with anyone else.

We wish you the best as you travel on your personal path to your destiny!

ASPIRE
SEMINARS

If you are interested in booking a speaking engagement with Sandra,
please contact Aspire Seminars.
We would love to send you information to help you decide
if Sandra would be a good fit for your event.

Phone: 360.539.9080
Toll Free: 866.788.0723
Email: Sandra@aspireseminars.com
Web site: www.aspireseminars.com

Your success is what we aspire to.

—Sandra Smith, President Aspire Seminars

ASPIRE
SEMINARS

Four Ways to Order!

1 **ONLINE:**
www.aspireseminars.com

3 **FAX ORDER FORM TO:**
866-826-8361

2 **CALL TOLL FREE:**
866-788-0723

4 **MAIL ORDER FORM TO:**
Aspire Seminars
P O Box 3603
Lacey, WA 98509-3603

SHIP TO:

NAME (please print)

ADDRESS

CITY   STATE   ZIP

PHONE   EMAIL
(We will call only if we have a question about your order)

Item#	Quantity	Description/Title	Amount

	Subtotal	
	WA Residents add 8.4% Tax	
($4 for first book, $2 each add'l book)	**Shipping**	
	Total	

PAYMENT INFORMATION:

☐ Check or Money Order (Payable to Aspire Seminars)

☐ Bill my credit card# _____

   ☐ Visa ☐ MC ☐ AmEx   Exp Date _____

                       Signature _____

☐ Purchase Order #: _____

Please allow 4-6 weeks for US delivery. Prices are subject to change without notice.

ASPIRE
SEMINARS
WWW.ASPIRESEMINARS.COM